Contents

—⁓—

Chapter One
Peace and Trouble—the Missing Link   1

Chapter Two
Welcome to Trouble
—and Deeper Intimacy with Jesus   20

Chapter Three
God's Agenda: Faithfulness, not Success   42

Chapter Four
The Trouble Is in Your Head   61

Chapter Five
You Really Do Have an Enemy   82

Chapter Six
The Hedge Is Down—the Stronghold Invaded   98

Chapter Seven
Walking in Faith and Discerning God's Will   114

Chapter Eight
You Can Rejoice in Trouble   132

Chapter Nine
The Joy of Repentance—the Lord's Invitation   149

Epilogue   167

Notes   169

The Truth About Trouble

HOW HARD TIMES CAN DRAW YOU CLOSER TO GOD

MICHAEL SCANLAN, T.O.R., WITH JIM MANNEY

SERVANT BOOKS

PUBLISHED BY ST. ANTHONY MESSENGER PRESS
CINCINNATI, OHIO

Most Scripture in this work has been translated from the Greek by Michael Scanlan, T.O.R. In several places, the author's translation agrees with that of the *New International Version*. The abbreviation NIV has been used in the text to indicate such agreement. Some Scripture is taken from the *New Revised Standard Version* (NRSV) copyright ©1989 by the Division of Christian Education of the National Council of Churches of Christ in the United States of America and used by permission. All rights reserved.

Cover design by Steve Eames
Book design by Phillips Robinette, O.F.M.

Library of Congress Cataloging-in-Publication Data

Scanlan, Michael, T.O.R.
  The truth about trouble : how hard times can draw you closer to God / Michael Scanlan, with James Manney.
        p. cm.
  Originally published: Ann Arbor, Mich. : Redeemer Books, c1989.
  ISBN 0-86716-621-5 (alk. paper)
  1. Suffering—Religious aspects—Christianity. 2. Spiritual life—Christianity. I. Manney, James D. II. Title.

BT732.7.S34 2005
248.8'6—dc22

                              2004030191
ISBN 0-86716-621-5

Published by Servant Books, an imprint of St. Anthony Messenger Press.
28 W. Liberty St.
Cincinnati, OH 45202
www.americancatholic.org

Previous edition published by Servant Publications.

Printed in the United States of America

Printed on acid-free paper

05 06 07 08 09 5 4 3 2 1

Chapter One

—⁓—

PEACE AND TROUBLE —THE MISSING LINK

Jesus couldn't have been any clearer about the trouble his followers would encounter. He was at times enigmatic about his identity, obscure about the precise nature of his kingdom, cryptic about his plans. But he spoke about trouble with crystal clarity: "In me you will have peace," he told his disciples. "In the world you will have trouble" (John 16:33).

This short sentence from the lips of our Lord and Savior contains the two most important truths about trouble. First, we *will* experience trouble; there's no escaping it. Second, and more importantly, "In me you will have peace."

These are not cause-and-effect statements: peace *causes* trouble, or trouble *brings* peace. Neither are they chronological statements: we have peace, *then* trouble; or trouble, *then* peace. Jesus said we have both peace and trouble together. Peace is not the absence of trouble; peace is the relationship we have with Jesus Christ, which deepens while we are going through trouble.

Christians know that suffering is redemptive, that by embracing the pain and trials in our lives, we unite ourselves with the saving suffering of Jesus. I will touch on this aspect of trouble from time to time, but it is far more skillfully handled elsewhere by the greatest spiritual writers. I want to write about a narrower question: the challenge of embracing both peace and trouble at the same time. This is one of the greatest challenges in the Christian life. It is also one that we all face almost all the time. In fact, embracing peace and trouble together is a good working definition of our daily walk as Christians.

WHAT I MEAN BY "TROUBLE"

The Irish, who are no strangers to suffering, have an expression that I often heard in my youth at times of sadness. We would be at a wake or in a cemetery following a graveside service. Irish family members and acquaintances would approach a newly-widowed woman, or parents who had just lost a child, and say, "I'm sorry for your trouble." The word "trouble" always struck me as way too mild to describe what the mourners were experiencing. "Desolation" seemed more fitting. How about misery?

I am using the word *trouble* in a somewhat similar way. It refers to a wide range of tribulations—from the disappointments and frustrations that annoy us to the tragedies and disasters that can devastate us. They are part of life. Indeed, they are so common that we often respond to a friend's litany of troubles by saying, "that's life."

Our troubles include our sufferings as our bodies are afflicted with disease and injury and as they wear out and break down with age. Some of the deepest and most painful troubles involve broken relationships—marriages that fail, wayward children, rancor in families, betrayal by friends. We can be bored, oppressed, sometimes bitterly disappointed by the work we do—work that we might think that *God* has given us to do. Some of our saddest troubles have to do with ourselves. We struggle ineffectively with persistent sin in our lives. We are afflicted with glaring weaknesses that we cannot change. We constantly fail to be as generous, as kind, as loving as we should be.

It could be worse. Much worse. Christians in Pakistan, Sudan, India, and other places are sometimes hunted down and killed. It's a good idea to periodically remind ourselves that the people who first heard Jesus say "in this world you will have trouble" had reason to fear for their lives because they were his followers. This is a reality for some Christians even today.

Still—the problems we face are real problems, and they really hurt. A Christian in Egypt may have worse troubles than we do, but it's usually not very helpful to point this out, any more than it's helpful to tell a depressed person to cheer up. Small troubles as well as large ones can grind us down, wear us out, extinguish our hope, and bring us to the edge of despair—and beyond.

FACING UP TO THE IDEA OF TROUBLE

The fact that relatively small troubles can grind us down points toward the most important truth about trouble. *Troubles will come. It's how we relate to them that matters.* This book is about thinking about troubles correctly, becoming spiritually equipped to deal with them effectively, and, in the end, learning how to use troubles as a means of deepening our relationship with God. The first step is to think about troubles the right way. The *idea* of trouble can give us lots of trouble. We latch onto the idea that things should be different than they are.

Christian Life as Utopia. Most of us know that sorrow and pain are part of our lives as Christians. But sometimes we have trouble believing that they should be such a *large* part of our lives.

This is especially true for those who have seen their life getting better after awakening to a new relationship with God. Most of us have had an experience like that. Life gets better when we get to know God better. We have a sharper sense of the Lord's presence, a renewed confidence in the future, a greater awareness of the Lord's love for us and for those we love. Perhaps you have turned away from bad relationships and serious sin and have experienced freedom and joy as a result. Although part of you knows better, it's tempting to think that it will be smooth sailing for the future.

"It ain't necessarily so," to quote a line from a song of my youth. The Christian life is not a highway to utopia, nor is it a blueprint for perfection. There are many clouds in the Christian sky.

When trouble comes, as it will, it can wreak havoc in this perfect world. The family crisis, the bankruptcy, the serious illness, can look like a terrible mistake, a shattering exception to the placid, smooth, and cheerful course of perfect lives in a perfect world.

The truth is that trouble will come. Jesus *means* it to come. The Christian life is not supposed to be trouble-free. Christians will never be perfect, and the point of growing as Christians is not to avoid difficulties and unpleasantness but to face them in the Lord.

The Comfort Gospel. Some Christians hold to what's called "the prosperity gospel." This is the belief that God rewards righteous people with material blessings —successful businesses and investments, nice homes, big new cars, vacations, and the other visible signs of worldly success. This idea even has some biblical support. The Hebrew people believed this for generations, until the facts of life and God's fuller revelation of himself superseded it.

It *is* hard to believe in the prosperity gospel as a principle of faith. Facts conflict with it: God does *not* seem to always bless the righteous with *evident* prosperity. The gospels clearly teach a different ethic, an ethic of love and service and of living for another kingdom. Certainly Jesus our Lord, the man whom we imitate, enjoyed no blessings of worldly success.

But it's not hard to slide into a "comfort gospel." God will take care of me. I'm not wealthy, just *comfortable*. Things aren't wonderful; they're just very good. I'm not always at the pinnacle of success; I'm just serene, enjoying the good things of God. "God wants it that way," we think.

It's especially easy to equate comfort and God in our North American society, which combines great wealth with a high degree of religiosity. Nevertheless, the "good life" in America is not the Christian life. Trouble will disturb the serenity of our lives. "God can't want it *that* way," we say. The comfort gospel can prevent us from seeing that he *does* want it that way.

God Will Deliver Me. A subtler mistake is to view hardship as essentially something that we will be delivered from. When we are weary and afflicted, when we're confronted with serious hardship, we say, "The Lord will deliver me."

He will, and he does—but rarely according to *our* timetable. Weeks, months, years can pass. Our loved one keeps on drinking, our son does not come back to the church, the depression doesn't lift. Prayer and fasting don't seem to make any difference. Where's the deliverer the psalms talk about? What's wrong with God?

Something *is* wrong—with us. Our troubles are not occasions for God to display his power. One of the axioms of the Christian life, one which I will repeat often in this book, is that troubles have much to teach us. Often the lesson is patience; sometimes it is humility. The Lord will deliver us according to *his* schedule, not ours. And when deliverance comes, it comes from his hand—not from our fervent prayers and heroic fasting.

Satan's Plan—For Me? Often our thinking about trouble doesn't take into account the reality of spiritual warfare. It's not hard to believe that malevolent evil forces are at loose in the world when we ponder events like the terrorist attacks of September 11, the near-assassination of the pope, and the horror of crimes of sexual abuse. But, in my experience, we have a harder time seeing the role of evil spiritual forces in our own humble lives. We are disinclined to believe that Satan *really* has a plan for us *personally*, a plan that he tries to execute. We are more likely to believe that troubles are caused by our defects, by God's lack of concern, or by circumstances.

But the truth is that the devil is real. That is the consistent teaching of the church through the ages. The church's accumulated pastoral wisdom testifies to the influence of evil spiritual forces on individuals. Careful discernment is called for here. Not all troubles are caused by Satan. We can make serious mistakes by seeing the devil everywhere and attributing powers to him that he simply doesn't have. But it's also true that we are involved in spiritual warfare. We are both the battleground and the army. The enemy wants to rob you of your salvation—*you*, personally. He knows you—not as well as God knows you, but he knows you.

Many of the troubles in our lives are battles in a lifelong spiritual conflict. We have the weapons to fight this war successfully. One of them is simple awareness that many troubles are caused not by us or by God or by circumstances, but by an enemy.

The Cancer of Discontent. Discontent is common. It's even admired. We think people are creative and energetic when they are not satisfied with things the way they are. Discontent leads to new ideas, hard work, greater productivity.

However, discontent in our spiritual lives can be poisonous. We get a certain kind of picture in our minds about what we want and what we're aiming for—a certain kind of marriage, a certain kind of family, a certain kind of job and service. When the reality is different from the picture, as it always is, we get discontented. This can eat away at our faith just as cancer destroys a human body. Discontent can also leave us unprepared to face real trouble when it comes.

The antidote to discontent is the person of Jesus Christ. Discontent comes from living our faith without centering it on the Lord. At the center of our Christian life is a person, a man like us in all things except sin. Our faith is not centered on rules, a pattern of life, a style of prayer, or our expectations.

We look to Jesus, and we seek what *he* wants to do in our lives.

THE SOMETIME CHRISTIAN

Late one afternoon I sat down in the Birmingham airport about as tired as I ever get. I had just taped a series of television shows at Mother Angelica's studios at the Eternal World Television Network. I was physically drained and mentally fatigued. Television can do that to you.

A man in the boarding area looked at me.

"Hi," he said.

"Hi, there."

"Are you a priest?"

"That's right." I had come from the television studio. I was wearing a Roman collar and a clerical suit, instead of my Franciscan habit.

"Where are you going?" he asked.

"Atlanta and Pittsburgh."

"So am I," he said.

I could see that I wasn't going to get much rest.

"Why don't you come over here and sit with me?" I asked. When he did, I decided not to waste any time.

"Are you a Christian? Have you given your life to Jesus Christ as your Lord and Savior?" I asked.

It turned out he had—several times. He had had religious experiences, but they just didn't seem to stick. He would go to church or to a prayer meeting and cry out to God for peace and assurance. And he would get what he asked for. Then he would encounter some trouble at work or at home, and the spiritual feeling he had would vanish. He'd conclude that God had abandoned him. That's why he wasn't sure how to respond when I asked him if he was a Christian.

I worked with this man for a good while right there in the airport. I concentrated on the role of trouble in his life. I explained that when troubles came to him, as they inevitably would, he had to meet them firmly, confidently, and patiently. Difficulties in life are the rule not the exception, I said. Jesus would stand with him in this struggle. At my invitation, the man declared his sorrow for his sins and made a renewed affirmation of faith in Jesus.

When we parted ways, he said he was a changed man, and he was sure things would be different now. I hope and pray that that's true. At least his thinking was different about the role of trouble in his life.

I have met many people like this man. Trouble comes, and they fold up. Their faith withers to a Sunday obligation or is reduced to a set of intellectual beliefs with little practical influence on life as it is lived. The faith takes on new meaning and life when they realize that being a Christian is not a golden parachute. It's not a way of bailing out of trials and difficulties, but rather a way of coping with them.

Let's contrast this man's attitude—which isn't all that unusual, by the way—with the words of Scripture. We read this in Sirach 2:

> My child, when you come to serve the Lord,
>   prepare yourself for testing.
> Set your heart right and be steadfast,
>   and do not be impetuous in time of calamity.
> Cling to him and do not depart,
>   so that your last days may be prosperous.

Accept whatever befalls you,
and in times of humiliation be patient.
(Sirach 2:1-4, NRSV)

Note the attitude here. The passage does *not* say, "those who don't come to the Lord will suffer crushing misfortunes." It says the opposite: "When you come to serve the Lord, prepare yourself for testing."

Sirach goes on to explain why testing is important for the person of faith: "For gold is tested in the fire, and those found acceptable, in the furnace of humiliation" (Sirach 2:5, NRSV). The metaphor here involves the method used to purify gold. Gold ore would be dug out of the ground with impurities in it. To extract the gold, the ore would be melted in a blazing hot fire, and pure gold skimmed away. In the same way, the righteous person is proven or tested in the crucible of humiliation. The defects are boiled away; what's left is the solid core of godly character.

What are we to think about this? Scripture has the answer to that too. "Rejoice about this, even though it may now be necessary for you to suffer for a while because of many kinds of trials," Peter writes. "Their purpose is to prove your faith genuine. Even gold which can be destroyed is tested by fire; so your faith, which is much more precious than gold, must also be tested so that it may endure" (1 Peter 1:6-7).

We don't have to be happy when trouble comes. But we can quietly rejoice at the opportunity it gives us to strengthen our faith and grow in Christian character.

It's often said that God *permits* suffering to befall us. This may not be the most theologically sophisticated way to put it. God does not author evil. The evils and afflictions of this world are the fruit of free human choices in a fallen creation. But, as one incident in the New Testament makes clear, God uses suffering. This is the story of one of Jesus' greatest miracles: the raising of Lazarus from the dead (see John 11).

Jesus was a close friend of Lazarus and Martha and Mary, his sisters. Jesus often stayed with Martha and Mary in Bethany when he came to nearby Jerusalem. The three were very close to Jesus. When Jesus heard that Lazarus had died, he wept.

And yet Jesus ignored the sisters' urgent messages to come when Lazarus fell ill. Martha and Mary could see Lazarus was dying. Imagine their grief when they realized how serious their brother's condition was. Imagine their confusion and distress when they realized that Jesus was not coming in answer to their pleas. For Jesus stayed where he was for two more days before he came to Bethany. He wanted to make sure that Lazarus was dead before he arrived!

There's no getting around it. Jesus deliberately let Martha and Mary suffer. He did it for a higher good, of course. But his first concern was not that Lazarus and his sisters have the smoothest sailing possible through life.

If Jesus let them suffer for the sake of a higher good, doesn't it stand to reason that the same is true today, that relieving our suffering might not be the most important thing on God's agenda?

Martha's reaction is interesting. When Jesus finally showed up in Bethany, after Lazarus had been buried, she was reproachful: "If you had been here, Lord, my brother would not have died" (John 11:21).

We can hear the rebuke in her remark, but notice the faith in it. She didn't doubt that Jesus would have saved her brother's life if he had been in Bethany—an extraordinary statement at a time when medical science did not exist and everybody knew that a man like Lazarus, seriously ill and dying, was obviously doomed.

But how like us. We too believe that the Lord can do extraordinary things for us, but we too tend to expect the Lord to work in the way *we* want. We usually expect him to work in the way that benefits us most directly. But he doesn't. Instead he promises suffering, and he seems to go out of his way to see that it happens.

We are his friends. Martha and Mary and Lazarus were his dear friends too.

PEACE AND TROUBLE—THE MISSING LINK

"In me you will have peace, but in the world you will have trouble" (John 16:33).

Let's look a little more deeply into this most important promise of Jesus. Jesus is saying that being a Christian involves trouble. But what *is* the connection between peace and trouble?

The link is Jesus. St. Augustine, perhaps the greatest of all the church fathers, said in one of his sermons that it is precisely because one is a Christian that "he is destined to suffer more in this world."[1]

Jesus is both the cause of our trouble and the solution to it. He was a man at serious odds with the world he lived in. He was widely misunderstood, even by his own followers. Even members of his own family thought he was foolish. The religious and political leaders of his land identified him as a dangerous troublemaker. They were not entirely wrong to think so. They got rid of him—or so they thought. This is the man whom we love, whom we seek to imitate—a man whom the world despised. It is thus no surprise that we are going to be despised too. As we grow to know Jesus better, we are going to find ourselves at odds with the world we live in.

Some Christians are at such odds with the world that they lose their lives. In the last century Christians were persecuted wholesale by Nazis and Communists. In recent years many Christians have been murdered by right-wing death squads in Latin America, by Hindu mobs in India, and by Islamic terrorists in Africa, the Middle East, and Asia. Most died for the "crime" of simply being a Christian. Others invited the rage of the powerful by protesting terrible injustice. Two outstanding modern martyrs who did this are Oscar Romero in El Salvador and Maximilian Kolbe in Nazi Germany. Archbishop Romero was killed by assassins for denouncing the evils of the government of El Salvador. Kolbe volunteered to take the place of a condemned man who had been sentenced to die in a starvation bunker in a Nazi concentration camp during World War II.

America is a much more comfortable place for Christians, but there is trouble here too. We're not entirely at home in our celebrity-saturated entertainment culture, or in an economic system that celebrates materialist excess. We can't share the assumption of many of our fellow citizens that personal freedom is the greatest of civic virtues. We are profoundly at odds with the assault on human life that has come with the legalization of abortion.

Our alienation from "business as usual" in America has grown deeper in the last several decades.

For many years the Judeo-Christian worldview was respected in our schools, hospitals, courts, and other social institutions. In some cases these institutions explicitly followed policies that can only be called biblical. Now things are different. Increasingly, an explicitly Christian perspective is not welcomed in the public square. In fact, the expression of Christian views in schools, in politics, and in the media is often regarded as a dangerous violation of the constitutional separation of church and state.

The fact is that for generations Christians have been protected from hostile forces by the hedge of a civic religion. Now the hedge is down. I am reminded of the discussion between God and Satan that begins the Book of Job. God was proud of the righteous Job. Satan said he was a good man because God had put a hedge around him to keep Satan away. God said, "Fine. I'll take the hedge down and let you have a shot at him." Satan did, as we know, and Job suffered tremendous losses. But Job withstood the onslaught and endured in his love for God.

Today the hedge is down, and Satan is taking his best shot at the church. May we endure in our love for God as Job did. One of the most important truths about trouble is that Christianity is a countercultural movement. We are never at home in the world. We will always be uncomfortable here, and we are going to suffer as a result. This seems to be built into the way things are.

Read these verses from 1 Corinthians carefully:

> God purposely chose what the world considers foolish in order to shame the wise, and he chose what the world considers weak in order to shame the powerful. He chose what the world looks down on and despises and thinks is nothing in order to destroy what the world thinks is important.
>
> (1 Corinthians 1:27-28)

Meditate on these verses. Pray them. We believe things that the wise men of the world think foolish. We behave in ways that the movers and shakers and the power brokers consider ineffectual and weak. We associate with those whom the world considers absurd and despicable. Why? *To reduce to nothing things that are.*

Jesus did what this passage from 1 Corinthians describes. He took the way of peace, weakness, and love in a world of war, power, and hate. He embraced suffering. He conquered the final enemy—death—by going to the heart of suffering, by becoming suffering. And we, his followers, will conquer our world by following our master into the heart of trouble.

Don't be enemies of the cross, Paul warns the Christians at Philippi (see Philippians 3:18). This warning is not directed to pagans persecuting the church but to Christians who were enduring this persecution. It's directed to us. Don't fight the troubles in your life. Don't resent the suffering. Don't resist God's plan for you. The cross is in it.

When we embrace the cross, we will understand James' mysterious saying: "Consider it pure joy when you are confronted with every kind of trial" (James 1:2).

That understanding can make all the difference in the world—between God's peace and quiet desperation.

Note: In the context of this book, we are excluding discussion of the special grace or vocation to be a victim through redemptive suffering.

Chapter Two

—ɯ—

WELCOME TO TROUBLE—AND
DEEPER INTIMACY WITH JESUS

The most important movement in Christianity in the past century has been the Pentecostal movement, or the charismatic renewal, as many Catholics call it. Hundreds of millions of Christians around the world have been touched by it. Christians of all denominations and theological traditions have had a "baptism of the Spirit"—the encounter with the Holy Spirit that is the hallmark of the Pentecostal experience.

While Pentecostal Christians share this experience, they have different ideas about what it means to be baptized in the Spirit. Some say the initial evidence is the charismatic gift of tongues. Others say it's an inner conviction that Jesus is with them in a new way. Some think there doesn't have to be a unique manifestation, that if you pray to be baptized in the Spirit, you are.

A friend of mine named Bob Mumford has a different idea. "The initial evidence of the baptism of the Spirit?" he asks. "That's easy. The initial evidence is trouble."

He's right. Those who take seriously the call to follow Jesus will encounter trouble: inner trouble—spiritual battles in our souls and spirits; outer trouble—conflict with other forces around us. It's part of the package.

It's like the trouble you get into when you join an army. I am amused by the television commercials for the armed forces. They promise glamour and success—excellent training in high-tech jobs, world travel, a snappy uniform, pride in a purpose. The commercials don't describe the other side of life in the armed forces. I remember my own years of duty in the Air Force. The work was often challenging, but much of life was dreary. We lived with stress and frustration. Conflicts erupted all the time when dozens of self-centered men lived together. Above all, there was boredom—the empty hours that no armed forces recruiting commercial will ever describe.

Often men would complain to their superiors about the difficulties. "The food is terrible," they would say, or, "I can't sleep in these lousy barracks," or, "I can't stand this Mickey Mouse paperwork."

The officers' reply would always be the same: "You signed up for it, buddy. This is the Air Force. It's all part of the contract."

IT'S NOT LIKE THE TV COMMERCIALS AT ALL

Most of us have a hard time seeing the analogy between being a Christian and being in an army. Soldiers have a uniform, a distinct identity, and a mission different from everyone around them. Christians are often unclear about their mission, and it's hard to tell the difference between Christians and everyone else. Yet the truth is that we have a communal identity, very much like that of soldiers. Our mission is to imitate Jesus as we live our lives and to be holy as he is holy. If we take this mission seriously, we will encounter conflict, frustration, and outright failure, as soldiers do. We learn things about ourselves that we'd rather not know.

But we signed up for it. Here is Jesus, the commander, telling his first recruits what awaits them as his followers. Here the captain is making a full disclosure:

> I send you out as sheep in the midst of wolves; so be wise as serpents and harmless as doves. Beware of men, for they will deliver you up to councils and flog you in their synagogues, and you will be dragged before governors and kings for my sake,

> to bear testimony before them and the Gentiles....
> Brother will deliver up brother to death, and the
> father his child, and children will rebel against
> parents and have them put to death; and you will
> be hated by all for my name's sake.
>
> (Matthew 10:16-18, 21-22)

To call these promises austere is an understatement. The requirements are no less imposing. We're to be both harmless and clever, good witnesses, free of anxiety, and faithful to the end. We don't hear much about Matthew 10 when we renew our baptismal vows, when we're confirmed, or when we go forward after a prayer meeting to be baptized in the Spirit. But it's part of the package. It's the life we sign up for.

ANNOYED AND AFFLICTED

There's a difference between annoyances and real troubles. Many of our daily troubles are basically annoyances. A harried driver cuts you off. You are forced to walk a few blocks in the rain. A waiter overcharges you in a restaurant. Even the relational conflicts and disappointments that sprinkle our lives rarely rank as serious trouble in the scriptural sense. "My daughter is sulking." "My boss won't listen to my ideas." "I'm so frustrated with my spouse."

These are real problems; they can hinder our walk with the Lord and interfere with our service to others.

But they are like batting practice—at best a warm-up for major-league conflict. If you are sold out for the Lord, if you stand for the gospel without compromise, you will experience real trouble.

I found myself in such a position in 1974 when I became president of the then College of Steubenville. I had a vision of what I thought the school should become. It wasn't even a well-thought-out plan; it was merely a strong sense of what the Lord wanted.

I thought the college should emphasize spiritual matters. Our priority should be to build up the theology department by teaching theology in conformity to the magisterium of the church. The students' spiritual well-being should be our first concern and have first call on our resources. Men and women should not live together in the dorms. The college should have nothing to do with immoral entertainment. Our attention should be on preparing young men and women to live a righteous and fruitful life. We should teach them how to date, how to raise a healthy Christian family, how to discern God's will, how to pray.

I thought this was a moderate, noncontroversial, "renewal-minded" vision for a Catholic college.

A great outcry greeted me—from students, of course, but also from parents, alumni, faculty, and even brother priests. All because I had just talked about some changes.

You will find yourself in a similar situation whenever you stand for your idea of the Lord's truth without compromise. It will happen even if you just talk about it. It will get worse when you do it.

Why? Because the gospel divides as well as liberates. When you proclaim it unambiguously and live it courageously, you will find yourself reviled and hated, hauled up before rulers, persecuted and despised. The gospel separates the sheep from the goats, those who have ears to hear from those who don't, and those with hearts of stone from those with hearts of flesh.

It's part of what we sign up for.

The first requirement is honesty. We have to see reality—and our situation—for what it really is. The late Father Jim Ferry, a veteran leader of the charismatic renewal, used to make this point with humor. He showed how our language masks what is really going on in people's lives.

Jim said that the remark "I'm having a desert experience" means that everything in the person's life has fallen apart. He or she feels alone and has no idea where to begin to put things back together.

"God is purifying me" means the Christian has been shocked and upset to discover a personal sin that he or she never expected to be there.

When we go to conferences where we are filled with the grace of renewal, it's "glory be to the Father and to the Son and to the Holy Spirit." When we return home, it's "as it was in the beginning, is now, and ever shall be, world without end."

There's exaggeration in his humor, but the point behind it is valid. The first step in dealing with the difficulties that afflict us is to honestly acknowledge that they exist. Don't deny them—to yourself or to others. Name them. Admit that they hurt. Acknowledge that you may not have the slightest idea how to solve the problems in your life. Recognize that you need help to endure what lies ahead.

Beware of euphemisms of the kind Jim Ferry gently made fun of. Euphemistic spiritual talk often gets in the way of a simple, honest acknowledgment of reality. Spiritual experience can often do the same. We can think of the spiritual life as a rocket launching. A good retreat or an experience like the baptism of the Spirit ignites a powerful engine. We roar into space with spectacular power. God is with us; who can hinder our way? First the moon, then the planets, tomorrow the stars. There's no limit to what can happen in our lives.

But I remember watching one of the first United States rockets take off not long after the Soviet Union launched *Sputnik*. The rocket sat there on the pad, poised for launch. The countdown went to zero. The engine ignited. Fire spewed forth. But the rocket didn't go anywhere. It fell over on the pad, exploded, and burned up.

It had all that power and didn't go anywhere.

We make a similar mistake if we mistake spiritual experience for holiness. A spiritual experience—intense as it might be—does not accomplish holiness.

FOUR COMMON REACTIONS TO TROUBLE

The question is, what do we do about it? Before looking at the good that trouble does, we need to discuss how *not* to react when trouble and suffering afflict our lives.

Is That All There Is? The first mistake is the one that I've just mentioned: the false notion that an intense spiritual experience will last forever and carry us through all troubles. The conversion experience, the encounter with God on a retreat, the baptism in the Holy Spirit, are wonderful experiences, but they are not complete in themselves. Unless we face up to trouble courageously and realistically, we will be crushed by disappointment.

Spiritual Schizophrenia. Many Christians live double lives. One is life as it actually is: a struggle with troubles of various kinds, a battle that leaves us weary, sorrowful, and, too often, defeated. The other life is the sunny, cheerful face we present to the world and, too often, to ourselves. On the outside we're smiling, telling ourselves and everyone else that everything's just fine. Inside we're screaming, wondering how we're going to get through the day. The problem is made worse by social pressure to look good in front of others. The fear of embarrassment and a reluctance not to burden others with our troubles are other reasons to keep up the cheery façade.

Giving Up. When a boxer is being beaten up badly, his manager can stop the fight by throwing a towel into the ring. Many Christians throw in the towel in the face of trouble. The sufferings are so painful, the gap between the ideal and reality is so great, that they surrender. They conclude that being a Christian has nothing to do with the disappointments, the relationship problems, the illnesses, the financial struggles that consume their energy and dominate their thoughts. It may work for others, we think, but I'm a hopeless case.

This is a not-so-subtle form of pride. It amounts to thinking that we're too bad a case for even God to save. Not even God's power is enough to change someone as uniquely afflicted or sinful as I am. It's important to see the pride in this response. The truth is that there is no sin or affliction bigger than God and his grace. Nothing can escape the saving power of his cross. To give up is never justified. It's never a solution to the troubles in our lives.

Willpower Christianity. The final unhelpful response to trouble is to try to overcome it on our own power. We redouble our efforts to persevere. We engage in various spiritual, mental, and physical disciplines. We'll work harder here, longer and more intensely there. God gave me life, we say, and he'll be there at the end to receive me. In the meantime, it's up to me to accomplish anything that's going to be accomplished.

This is another form of pride. It focuses on the self and leaves out the power of God and the power of his cross.

A TIME-CONSUMING PROCESS

These four wrong responses to trouble and affliction all ignore a great truth about life in the Spirit. The great key is this: *Conversion is a process that takes time.* We can have many experiences of God, but sanctification is something that goes on for a long time. Trials and difficulties become opportunities to mature in the Lord. As we do mature, we realize that God's provision is far greater than we can anticipate or even imagine.

We need to believe what God says about us rather than what we say about ourselves. We hear God speaking about us all through Scripture. How are we to take this? The apostle James tells us at the beginning of his letter:

> Do not merely be hearers of the word and thereby deceive yourselves. Do what it says. Anyone who listens to the word but does not do what it says is like a man who looks at his face in a mirror and

> after looking at himself goes away and immediately forgets what he looks like. (James 1:22-23)

Sounds like a passage to give comfort to "willpower Christians," right? Wrong. James is saying that we find our true selves in God's Word. There God tells us who we are, who he is, what his standards are, and what his plan for us is. When we read God's Word we look at our true selves as in a mirror. We are men and women beloved of God, whom he has destined to spend eternity with him, whom he has saved by the sacrifice of his Son, whom he created in his own image, whom he loves so much that he offers us forgiveness for our sins and the power to become holy like him. "Doing what the Word says" means acting in accordance with what it says about who we are.

To act in accordance with what we think we are or with what other people think us to be is to act like a man who turns away from the mirror and immediately forgets what he looks like. Yes, we sin. Yes, we struggle with our afflictions and fall short of the holiness we aspire to. Yes, our resources are puny compared to the tasks set before us. But to focus on the struggle and the failure is to forget who we are. Look in the mirror again. See yourself as God sees you.

Paul did. He wrote:

> I do not do the good I want, but the evil I do not want is what I do.... I find it to be a law that when I want to do right, evil is present. For I delight in the law of God, in my inmost self, but I see in my members another law at war with the law of my mind and taking me captive to the law of sin which dwells in my members. (Romans 7:19, 21-23)

There is no better description of the dilemma we find ourselves in—creatures desiring to do good but seemingly condemned to do evil. But Paul looked in the mirror, and he saw who he really was and what God had done for him.

"There is therefore now no condemnation for those who are in Christ Jesus," he continued in Romans. "For the law of the Spirit of life in Christ Jesus set me free from the law of sin and death" (Romans 8:1-2).

How does this law of freedom come about in our lives? Gradually. More slowly than we like. Through a process.

"We know that the whole creation has been groaning in labor pains until now," Paul writes. "Not only the creation, but we ourselves, who have the first fruits of the Spirit, groan inwardly while we wait for adoption, the redemption of our bodies." He concludes: "But if we hope for what we do not see, we wait for it with patience" (Romans 8:22-23, 25, NRSV).

Paul says it authoritatively: everywhere that God is working the process of conversion is apparent. Paul sees this process in himself. He is in the midst of a process of conversion and growth. He holds on to the fullness of Jesus in hope, and in the meantime, he groans inwardly as he waits for the redemption of the body.

WHY HOLINESS REQUIRES TROUBLE

We are converted to Jesus Christ when we are baptized. Yet our conversion to him is unfinished until we come to him at the end. Ongoing conversion is something we do every day.

One of the clearest statements of the need for ongoing conversion to Jesus was made in 1979 by Pope John Paul II, in a letter addressed to all the priests of the world. The Holy Father is a man without illusions. Unlike many previous popes, he spent most of his life as a parish priest and then as a diocesan bishop intimately acquainted with many priests in ordinary parish ministry. He knows the loneliness of priestly life, its frustrations, its meager rewards in worldly terms, its special dangers and temptations. His letter to priests can also be applied to the person who lives out his vocation in the world—groaning while we wait for the fullness of redemption.

Pope John Paul called for daily conversion among priests. "We must all be converted anew every day," he said. "If we have the duty of helping others to be converted we have to do the same continuously in our own lives."[1]

He goes on to give five meanings of conversion:

> Being converted means returning to the very grace of our vocation; it means meditating upon the infinite goodness and love of Christ, who has addressed each of us and, calling us by name, has said: "Follow me." Being converted means continually "giving an account before the Lord of our hearts about our service, our zeal and our fidelity, for we are "Christ's servants, stewards entrusted with the mysteries of God." Being converted also means continually "giving an account" of our negligent behavior and our sins, of our timidity, of our lack of faith and hope, of our thinking only "in a human way" and not "in a divine way".... Being converted means, for us, seeking again the pardon and strength of God in the sacrament of reconciliation, and thus always beginning anew.... Being converted [means] "to pray continually and never lose heart."[2]

There it is, the demands of daily conversion. It's not a vague "spiritual" process. It's very concrete, very specific, very honest. Daily conversion, according to the pope, means a daily recommitment to our vocation as sons and daughters of God, placing ourselves daily in Christ's infinite love and goodness, giving an account of our work, giving an account of our failures, and praying daily without losing heart. This process of conversion assumes that we will fail. It assumes that our loyalty and commitment will be tested every day. It assumes that we need help.

That is, perhaps, the greatest truth about trouble. Conversion is something that takes place in our failure and weakness. Our sin is not an impediment to the process; conversion requires sin. God is constantly making us over into the men and women he wants us to be. He wants to change those root desires that lead us to sin. He wants to sweep away the confusion in our minds. He wants to soften our hard hearts.

There lies our joy. It's the joy of being constantly renewed by the power of the cross, of coming again and again to Jesus as our Savior, of placing our trust in him and knowing that he is our all.

That's how we are to understand perhaps Jesus' most difficult words. Mark renders them, "If you believe, you will receive everything you ask for in prayer" (Mark 11:24). Matthew has them: "You will receive all that you pray for provided you have faith" (Matthew 21:22). Who has not scratched his or her head over these passages, or squirmed in church at their reading?

What God is after is not the promise of a magical method of prayer that will give us whatever we want.

He's talking about building a relationship with him such that we are one with him. More precisely, he's after restoring a relationship that humans once had with him.

The first chapters of Genesis describe this relationship between God and the first man and woman (Genesis 2:15ff.; 3:8ff.). Adam and Eve actually walked and talked with God in the garden. We can visualize the intimacy of the relationship. Adam and Eve saying, "This is what we did today, and this is what needs fixing up in the garden, and this is what we plan to do about it." God listens intently, then says, "Fine, now here's something else I want you to take care of, and this is how to do it."

Conversion is restoring this relationship. God can do it only as we allow him to. Much within us obscures his voice and destroys the relationship. But this intimacy is what he is after, and what he will one day achieve.

We *can* have intimacy with God. We can hear his voice every day and rely on his provision for us. One man who did was George Müller, a nineteenth-century British Protestant who had a special call from God to take care of orphans.

GEORGE MÜLLER AND THE ORPHANS

Müller kept things very simple. He went to the Lord every day in prayer and asked, "Lord, what do you want me to do?" Orphans and homeless people came to him, first one, then two, then a flood. Each day Müller would say to the Lord, "Lord God, you are calling me to care for these orphans. I trust you to provide for us."

Often Müller would take in orphans when he had nothing—no money, no room, no food. Stories are told about his legendary faith. Sometimes, with no food in the house and no prospect of getting any, he would set the table for dinner and sit down with his orphans and wait. He never had to wait more than twenty minutes before someone arrived with food.

Müller took care of more than 126,000 people in his long life. Some ten thousand of them were orphans. He took care of them through prayer—through God's provision, not his own.

Müller kept a journal in which he listed his needs and what he heard God say about how each need was to be fulfilled. When the need was met, he would note it in his journal. At his death at the age of ninety-three, his journal had more than fifty thousand entries of answered prayer.

Müller knew that most people didn't approach God in the simple way that he did. In one of his journals he says that the biggest problem we have in relying on God's provision for our lives is the bondage of our hearts. Deep down, we want to run the universe. We want our needs taken care of. We want our plan to unfold in our lives. We need to be free before God, to trust him more than we trust ourselves.

In Philippians Paul prays that "God will meet all your needs according to his glorious riches in Christ Jesus" (4:19). Note the phrase "according to his glorious riches in Christ Jesus." It's not according to your needs, according to your merits, according to how good you've been, how strong you are, or how hard you work, not according to what kind of friends you have or commitments you've made. It's *according to the riches in Christ Jesus*. He is our fund and foundation. He is our treasury.

And so we must keep our eyes fixed on Christ Jesus. Our needs will be met according to the glorious riches in him, so how can we go wrong? He says, "Look to me. I will tell you what to do and where to go. I will supply what you need." How can we refuse him?

We can and do. Following Jesus with an empty and trusting heart involves a kind of death. Death, in fact, is what Scripture calls it. "Whoever wants to save his life will lose it, but whoever loses his life for my sake will find it" (Matthew 16:25). Some Christians will literally die for the Lord. All of us must die to the "self"—that core of our unredeemed personality that pushes us forward to satisfy our own desires. If we hang on to the self, we will die the eternal death. But if we give the self up, emptying our hearts, we will live forever.

THE LESSON OF A BROKEN COLLARBONE

Often adversity teaches us how to live as Christ wants.

Several years ago I was riding a bicycle for some exercise during a break in a conference. I tried to make a turn too tightly, skidded on some gravel, and crashed into the ground. I broke my collarbone.

Medical science can't do much about broken collarbones. The doctors strapped me up, gave me some painkillers, and sent me home. I recovered very slowly. Adhesions formed in the shoulder; they had to be broken by painful manipulation. I wasn't sick enough not to work, but I wasn't able to work effectively. I can see now that I rushed things. I tried to return to normal activity too quickly.

Soon I was in trouble. I was constantly tired, at times very distracted by pain or mentally impeded by pain-killing drugs. I had little energy. I could push myself to get through perhaps one demanding task a day before I would retire to my bed in exhaustion. I made thoughtless and embarrassing lapses. I would forget appointments, break commitments, drift in and out of conversations. It was a humbling affliction for someone who was supposed to be giving leadership.

In this trouble I meditated on the verse from Hebrews: "Let us fix our eyes on Jesus, the author and perfecter of our faith" (12:2). I tried to look at Jesus more intently than I had ever done. I found that I could identify with him—the suffering Jesus, the obedient Jesus, the dying Jesus, the resurrected Jesus. I found that he gave meaning to my life when I was confused, in pain, and in the grip of forces I could not control.

Paradoxically, with many of my faculties impaired, I could see the important things more clearly. The most important thing is that Jesus loves us and died for us. He took on the weakness of the human condition and submitted to the abuses of men in order to restore us to intimacy with God. Because of him it is once again possible for men and women to walk with their Father in the garden, as the first man and woman did.

I found out, as Paul writes in Romans 8, that neither life nor death nor anything else—pain, painkillers, exhaustion, or confusion—could separate me from the love of God in Christ Jesus. I reached bottom, and Jesus was there. Here is a word from the Lord which I wrote in my journal when I was at my low point: "Now you are broken and helpless. You can't possibly continue as you have in the past. Now I will show you my ministry, and all you have been doing will be organized around it. You are sufficiently out of the way, with your eyes seeking me, for me to move with my ministry, unmistakably marked with my character."

This word reminded me of an anecdote from Archbishop Alban Goodier's book *A More Excellent Way*. The archbishop tells how he devised a plan to get holy when he was a zealous young seminarian. He chose the twelve most important virtues of the Christian life and resolved to work on one during each month of the year.

> When I was younger, a novice in religion, and knew myself less, and knew others less, and was full of high ambitions in the spiritual life, and sought in books and in study, in thought-out plans and schemes on paper for guides to the summit of perfection, I set virtues before me and meditated on their beauty and proposed to myself to acquire them, subdividing them, analyzing them, arranging their degrees as the steps of a ladder.
>
> This week, as the good spiritual writers bade me, I would acquire the virtue of patience; next week it should be a carefully guarded tongue; the week after should be given to charity; then should come the spirit of prayer; and in a month or two, perhaps, I might have an ecstasy and "see the Lord." But now, when I have grown older, and find myself still struggling for the first of these virtues, and that in a very elementary degree, and have been taught quite other lessons than I dreamt of, in part by the sorry disappointments in my own soul, in part by the progress seen in the souls of others, I am convinced that there is one road to perfection better than all else—in fact, that if we neglect this one, no other will be of much avail.[3]

This more excellent way is Jesus. He is the fullness of God. He is the beginning and the end. We meet him in our triumphs and joys. We especially meet him in our weakness and trouble. We are destined to live forever with him. In the meantime, he will meet our needs according to his great riches.

However, we are certain to learn the same lesson Archbishop Goodier learned: God will meet our needs in ways we do not expect. We will face the most terrifying lesson of all: success lies in what everyone else thinks is failure.

Chapter Three

—\\\\—

God's Agenda:
Faithfulness, not Success

How do we live the Christian life? This question constantly presents itself. Our faith is in part a way of thinking and a set of doctrines. It's important to understand these ideas, and we can spend many hours and much energy on learning, but living the Christian life does not consist of study. Our faith also involves experience of God. At various times in our lives we come to taste deeply of God's love for us, and we experience the leading of the Holy Spirit. But spiritual experience fades in intensity. Life looks pretty much the way it always has. It's tough. People are selfish and sad and distant. They do things that are not good for them. Worse, they do things that we don't think are good for us.

More to the point, we discover that we are imperfect. We are selfish and sad and distant. We do things that are not good for us, and we do things to other people that are not good for them. We confront the truth that we are sinners. We find ourselves "doing the things we hate" (see Romans 7:15).

Our faith involves work—both in the church and in the world. The possibilities are endless. We can go to the parish ministry fair and throw ourselves into the liturgy, choir, social action, youth program, and a myriad of other activities. We can fight against abortion, join a prison ministry, volunteer for the soup kitchen or homeless shelter.

But we discover that we work in mixed and imperfect situations. Some of the most mixed and imperfect situations involve work with other Christians who are sincerely and intelligently trying to serve the Lord together. In a secular business harsh disagreements can erupt over how best to make money. In the church bitter conflicts can arise over how best to serve the Lord.

Welcome to reality, the cynics say. The ideal of the kingdom of God cannot be attained on this earth. It's the fate of faithful Christians to drink deeply from the cup of sorrow.

So how do we live the Christian life?

Modern Christianity is full of priests and preachers and writers and counselors who deal with this question. Much of what they say is useful. Any one of us could profitably spend years listening to their tapes and reading their books. (In fact, study and training should never end. They should be a feature of every serious Christian's life.)

I want to focus on one part of the answer. It's only a part, but it's an important part and, I think, a neglected part. It has to do with faithfulness.

FAITHFULNESS, NOT SUCCESS

I believe that faithfulness makes the difference between being given over to God and being used by God. It's very possible to love God, to believe the right things about him, even to do many splendid things for him, and still to follow our own path instead of his. It's possible to follow the Lord for a time and then give up, to think that diligent, humble work in the service of the kingdom is something we do when we are young, or when we have time, or when we get in the right situation. It's possible to work for the Lord on our terms, not his.

My friend Chuck Colson, the founder of Prison Fellowship, has a plaque on his desk that says, "Faithfulness, Not Success"—a motto made famous by Mother Teresa. As she explained, and as Chuck Colson believes, the goal is faithfulness to our Father's word, faithfulness to our call and to the work he has given us to do. Success is God's business.

What does this have to do with the question "How do we live the Christian life?" It has to do with the quality that can do more than anything else to motivate us to humble, creative faithfulness. That motive is fear of the Lord.

That's right. Fear. Fear is not a popular topic in Christian circles these days (if indeed it was ever popular in any circles at any time). People don't like to think about fearing things, especially when it comes to religion. "Christianity is about love and not fear," we are told.

It's true that perfect love casts out all fear, but it's also true that we are supposed to develop a healthy fear of the Lord. The Scriptures are full of passages about fear of the Lord. They speak about the benefits of fear, one of which is that it frees us from other fears. The Bible says we are to grow in fear of the Lord and to live our daily lives in fear of him.

What kind of fear is this? If perfect love casts out all fear, how are we supposed to fear the Lord? An important clue comes from Psalm 147:11: "The Lord delights in those who fear him, who trust in his unfailing love." The psalms often employ repetition; the second part of a verse restates the meaning of the first part in a slightly different way. Here the meaning seems to be that there is a connection between fearing the Lord and trusting in his love. We don't fear in the sense that we cower in the corner waiting for God to catch us in some wrongdoing. Rather, we fear not being faithful to him. We fear having the relationship ruptured. We fear being separated from him.

Our human relationships offer a good analogy. What do we fear in marriage and in families? We fear something that will break up the relationship. The hard work we do to care for our children and strengthen our marriages is motivated in large part by fear—fear in the sense that we desire to avoid the consequences of failing to put in the necessary effort. This is the way love operates. We fear losing the one we love. We fear not acting respectfully and rightly. We fear being unfaithful.

Whenever I think of serving the great King, I recall an unusual and humorous encounter with earthly royalty I had many years ago. More precisely, it was a near encounter.

A BLOODY EMBARRASSMENT

The year was 1957. I was an officer in the Air Force and a lawyer on the staff of the Judge Advocate. Several other young lawyers and I hitched a ride on a military aircraft from Andrews Air Force Base in Washington, D.C., to London to attend a meeting of the American Bar

Association. The most powerful and prestigious lawyers and judges from the United States went to this meeting. The British legal establishment had gone to great lengths to welcome their American colleagues and to treat them as the honored professionals they considered themselves to be.

When we approached the registration table, we were told that we were invited each evening to a social event; but since we were so low on the priority or seniority list, our events would involve long travel to remote areas. I asked, "What should we do?"

The registrar responded, "Don't register. Present yourselves to the social events you choose. You look good in your uniforms and the Londoners will invite you personally."

It worked. The first night we went to an elegant reception hosted by a well-known socialite. The second evening we were welcomed into a reception by the Lord Mayor of London. The third night it was a party at the House of Lords. The British hosts were delighted to give hospitality to young American lawyers in military uniforms.

On the morning of the fourth day there was an announcement that Queen Elizabeth would receive the senior American lawyers at a special reception at Buckingham Palace. Needless to say, we wanted to go. Needless to say, admission was by invitation only.

Needless to say, we couldn't get invitations but went over to the palace anyway.

As we walked toward the palace gates in our Air Force uniforms and little black bow ties, a man in a limousine spotted us. It was the American Undersecretary of State, a man whom we had met at each of the previous receptions. He told us to climb in. We did. The undersecretary's invitation was taped to the windshield of the car. The guard waved the limousine through the first security check, then through the second check, and the third. We parked in a VIP space very close to the palace and were whisked inside along with the Very Important Person who had given us a lift.

We were delighted. We got in line to see the queen. We were smiling and happy and exceedingly pleased with ourselves.

Then a very large butler approached and said, "Your invitation, please."

"I'm sorry, but I'm not able to give you an invitation," I said.

The undersecretary turned around and said to the butler, "Oh, don't worry about it. I know these fellows. I'll vouch for them."

But suddenly I was filled with fear—not fear that I might be arrested or embarrassed, but fear that I was not acting in an honorable and respectful way. At the other parties I had been invited in. Here I really didn't belong. I had snuck in. If I was going to see the queen, it would be under false pretenses. I recalled Jesus' parable about the wedding guests who had been excluded from the feast because they weren't dressed appropriately. I realized I was an interloper. It wasn't right that I should see the queen.

Our gate-crashing ended swiftly and humorously. The butler turned us over to Scotland Yard agents standing nearby; they hustled us into a room and questioned us.

"It's a bloody embarrassment to us to have you get this far without an invitation," one of them said angrily.

They ushered us out the door of Buckingham Palace. A large crowd of Londoners was gathered there watching the famous American lawyers and the great British barristers. As the Scotland Yard agents ejected us into the street, we waved at the crowd. The people cheered and waved back, no doubt thinking that we were honored Americans who had to leave early.

I felt that I had acted dishonorably. It would have been wrong to approach the queen pretending to be something I wasn't.

I often feel the same way when I think about serving the Lord. I don't want any pretense or dishonesty between us. He is too great, too holy. I respect him too much.

That is the heart of fear of the Lord.

FEARING THE RIGHT THINGS

Fear is actually one of the most common human emotions. I have met many people who prided themselves on being fearless, but everyone is afraid of something, usually many things. We're afraid of losing our money, of not being successful, of sickness, of death. Most people fear not looking good in the eyes of other people. Some people are afflicted with neurotic fears of flying, of heights, of the dark, of crowds, of enclosed spaces.

Fear is rooted in our humanness. We are dependent creatures afflicted with a drive to be independent. We want to control everything, but life is outside of our control. We depend on other people. We depend on our unreliable selves. We depend on God.

We also fear because we love. Whatever we love we fear losing. Some of the things we love are fleeting and relatively unimportant—money, job, car, good looks. Some good things are more substantial and more important—our health, our lives, the lives of our loved ones. The only time we don't fear is when we aren't committed to anything.

Thus, a large part of spiritual maturity and emotional health consists of sorting out what we should fear and what we shouldn't. Jesus' words on the subject contain the key. He told us not to fear what men can do to you: how they steal from you or punish you or laugh at you. Rather, fear him who can take away eternal life (see Luke 12:4-5).

Many of us have it backward. We don't fear Satan and sin enough; we fear men and what they can do too much. Tragically, we can usually do very little about the things we fear. We can't control the ups and downs of the economy, the opinions of other people, who gets cancer, and the timing of our deaths. But we can control the degree to which we renounce Satan and are faithful to God.

Jesus told us something else about fear—that fear of the Lord banishes other fears. If fear afflicts you, you are probably afraid of the wrong things. The solution is to adopt the right kind of fear.

THE ALGEBRA TEST

I learned something of this when I was a boy in high school. Nobody taught me this lesson about fear; it was something the Lord showed me without any human intermediary.

My problem was algebra. Until I got to high school, I was on top of every subject in school. I always got good grades. Then, like many thousands of other students, something bad happened inside my head when the teachers put letters with the numbers. I had a hard time following the teacher. I sweated every night over algebra. As the final exam approached, I spent more time on algebra than on everything else put together.

Exam day came. The teacher passed out the tests. I looked at my exam—and froze. My mind blanked. I remembered nothing of what I had been taught about algebra. I was paralyzed by an overwhelming fear that nothing I did on this test was going to do me any good.

Not much of it did. I flunked the exam. It was the first examination I had ever failed.

That night I decided that what had happened was ridiculous. I had somehow gotten out of the Lord's plan for me and algebra. I had overprepared, panicked in great fear, and failed.

"What's there to be afraid of?" I thought. "The only thing worth fearing is being separated from the Lord. Getting upset over algebra is just stupid."

I resolved in the future to do just what the Lord wanted me to do to prepare for tests and to do only that much. Never again was I gripped with fear when I took a test, even tests as important as the New York Bar Exam and my final comprehensives to become a priest.

I've tried to apply the same principle to other work in my life. For many years I was president of a university. Every day I would come into the office and face at least two dozen problems clamoring for my attention. Student problems, faculty problems, administrative problems, urgent questions, pressing decisions that have to be made. Then I would step back from the immediate crises and survey what needed to be done in the next month or next year. I would easily list a hundred things I had to pay attention to.

In the face of all this, I made it my practice to ask: What does the Lord want me to do now? What do I have to do to be faithful to him today? He invariably showed me. I managed to get my work done. I didn't always do everything as quickly or as efficiently as other people wanted, and often other people had a different idea about what I should be doing at any particular time. But I stuck to the task of satisfying the one master who had given me this work to do. I respected him too much to do otherwise. I was too hesitant to please anyone but him. That attitude is fear of the Lord.

Sometimes the Lord's answers to that daily question "What shall I do now?" bring me face-to-face with other fears that I didn't even know I had.

I have loved preaching ever since I was ordained a priest. I preach as often as I can. When I was president of Franciscan University, I tried to preach every day on one of the Scripture readings from that day's Mass. I was good at this, and many people who listened to my homilies thought I was good at it too.

However, I was vaguely aware of one problem. I had a tendency to avoid the harder passages from the Bible and to preach on texts that had a more pleasing sound. The readings for the day usually gave me a choice. For my homily I would usually pick the reading that would seem least threatening and harsh to those who listened to me.

One Sunday I sensed that I should preach on a reading that was one of the least-pleasing passages in the Bible, especially on a college campus. It was 1 Corinthians 6:9-11, which reads:

> Do you not know that wrongdoers will not inherit the kingdom of God? Do not be deceived! Fornicators, idolaters, adulterers, male prostitutes, sodomites, thieves, the greedy, drunkards, revilers, robbers—none of these will inherit the kingdom of God. And this is what some of you used to be. But you were washed, you were sanctified, you were justified in the name of the Lord Jesus Christ and in the Spirit of our God. (NRSV)

I was supposed to preach on this text to a congregation of students. People listening to me could be found in all of Paul's categories of people who wouldn't inherit the kingdom of God. I was supposed to tell them that. I looked for some alternatives, but I couldn't find any. The master wanted me to deliver the hard word. Because I feared him, I obeyed.

So I stood before the congregation that Sunday and said, "I am going to tell you what the word of God says about immoral sexual activity, because I know that is the part you are most concerned about." I didn't just use 1 Corinthians 6:9-11. I went through the Old and New Testaments and summarized God's judgment on an immoral sexual life. I said that I wouldn't judge them but that God would, and that this was the standard he would use on the last day.

I did this out of obedience and fear of the Lord. To do it I had to confront some inner fears—fears of being rejected, fears of not being liked, fears of saying the wrong thing. But my fear of the Lord was strong enough to overcome these fears. I actually found it rather easy to stand up there and deliver one of the toughest sermons those young people had ever heard.

Their reaction caught me completely by surprise. The congregation was deadly quiet when I finished, but as I walked away from the pulpit there was a burst of applause. By the time I got back to my chair, everyone in the place was standing and clapping. Later I asked why. The students said, "No one ever said it that clearly before. We needed to hear what God expects. Now we know what to do."

What a lesson that was. It illustrates another spiritual principle: faithfulness brings forth good fruit. Fear of the Lord is not an abstract virtue that is rewarded at the end of time. It bears fruit in our lives and in the lives of others. It's as real as God himself.

WATCH THE MASTER'S HANDS

If security and fruitfulness lie in doing God's will, then how do we know what God wants of us?

That's the question we all ask. The history of the church is a mix of good and bad responses to that very question. That's what much of spiritual direction is all about. That's what much of our prayer is all about. The question seems more complicated today than it ever was because the options are so plentiful. Should we serve in our parish or should we look to some national or international ministry? To whom should we contribute money? How do we sort out conflicting priorities in our lives?

This is not the time to review everything we know about discerning God's will. But I would like to emphasize the role that fear has in the process. It is an important and often neglected role. God rarely shouts at us. He is more persistent than loud. We need to be attentive, watchful, sensitive to the leadings of his Spirit. We are far more likely to hear what he is saying if we have a healthy respect for him than if we take him for granted.

Psalm 123 says:

> As the eyes of servants
>   look to the hand of their master,
> as the eyes of a maid
>   to the hand of her mistress,
> so our eyes look to the Lord our God.
>
> (Psalm 123:2, NRSV)

In modern North America we don't have much first-hand experience with a servant's attentiveness to his master's direction, but it's not hard to picture. Imagine a large and elegant dinner party. The host has much to be concerned about as he sees to his guests' comfort. His servant stands nearby, watching, waiting for his instructions, his eyes fixed on his master's hands.

The master makes a small gesture. The servant takes a guest's coat. The master points. The servant has the musicians start to play. Another gesture. Plates are cleared and the next course is served.

We don't see this kind of attentiveness to authority very often in a democracy, where no one is supposed to be "better" than anyone else. However, once in my life I saw it up close. I was the servant. My master was the United States Attorney for the Southern District of New York.

I was a law student at the time, working a summer job as a legal assistant to an Assistant United States Attorney. He had assigned me to do research on a legal problem involving a notorious criminal named Trigger Burke.

Trigger Burke was the most famous mob gunman of the forties and fifties. He was known all over the East Coast as a ruthless hit man. He liked to use a machine gun on his victims; he would pull out the gun, flip his trigger finger, and a stream of bullets would cut down whomever he was assigned to kill.

FBI agents had arrested Burke on the boardwalk in Atlantic City. He was wanted by federal and state authorities and by the police of several cities. The problem was that the only federal crime he would be charged with was crossing state lines to avoid arrest—a relatively trivial offense. My bosses had decided that they wanted to turn Burke over to the local jurisdiction in Brooklyn, where he could be tried for murder. My assignment was to research the law and come up with a legal way to do that.

I did my job and turned in my work. When the big day came, I went down to the federal courtroom to watch Burke's arraignment.

It was a sensational event. The courtroom was packed with reporters. Television cameras and radio reporters were outside. Trigger Burke sat at the defendant's table with his lawyers, looking mean. The United States Attorney personally argued the case to turn Burke over to Brooklyn. I stood against the back wall, the least important person in the room.

Then, in the middle of arguments, the United States Attorney shuffled some papers in front of him, turned around, and saw me in the back. He flicked his index finger, summoning me. With the eyes of everyone on me, I walked forward to my boss's boss and answered a legal question he had about how the law applied in the Trigger Burke case. In essence, I explained how previous court decisions strengthened our argument that Burke could be turned over to the Brooklyn authorities.

It was a heady moment. Who knows what would have happened if I had been out at the water cooler instead of watching the United States Attorney.

Our case was successful. Trigger Burke went over to Brooklyn, where he was tried for murder and convicted. I experienced being completely under the command of one person, attentive to his every wish, part of an organization totally devoted to one goal: bringing a dangerous criminal to justice. I experienced the greatest professional usefulness that I had ever experienced until then, and it really was a small thing, a matter of answering one question. But I was able to do what may have been crucial because I was prepared, I was attentive, and I was watching my master's hand.

The task is similar in the kingdom of God. We need to be looking for the slightest inspiration of the Holy Spirit. We need to be listening for his voice in the Scriptures. We need to find out what God is saying in the spiritual books we read. We need to listen carefully for God's voice for us in sermons and homilies. We need to ask the Lord each day, "What do you want me to do? How do you want me to change? How should I repent?

What should I do differently? How can I serve you?"

Jesus said, "Seek first the kingdom of God and his righteousness, and all else will be given to you" (Matthew 6:33). That's what fear of the Lord is all about—seeking first the kingdom of God, seeing what God wants, seeking first the respect of God and not the respect of men.

We need to be able to say, "If men don't respect me but God does, then that's enough." That's fear of the Lord, and that is the key to being faithful.

Chapter Four

—⟋⟍—

THE TROUBLE IS IN YOUR HEAD

One spring afternoon C. S. Lewis was working at his desk when a friend who was visiting told him about a man's grave with an unusual epitaph.

"It was the tomb of an atheist," he said. "The epitaph read, 'Here lies an atheist. All dressed up and nowhere to go.'"

Instantly Lewis replied, "I'll bet he wishes *that* were so!"[1]

Another time Lewis and several students were reading and commenting on the poetry of World War I. Poem after poem lamented the tragic deaths of young men, cut down in the prime of their lives. As the discussion was winding down, Lewis made a startling remark.

"None of these poets points out that these young men would have died eventually anyway."[2]

Of course Lewis was right. The atheist's epitaph isn't all that funny when considered from an eternal perspective. Neither is premature death such a cosmic tragedy when we remember that we'll all die anyway, and that the important question is where we will spend eternity.

A century ago many people would have understood that. When thinking about death, Christian men and women would have thought about it the way Christ did. Europe and North America were deeply influenced by Christian culture.

C. S. Lewis thought with a classic Christian mind. His perspective was saturated with the mind of Christ—with the perspective of heaven and hell, the need for salvation, the wonder of the incarnation, gratitude for Christ's death and resurrection, and the assurance of the vanity of human enterprises compared to the eternal value of the kingdom of God.

His perspective seems startlingly novel. People rarely think this way today, especially when they are dealing with "secular" subjects such as politics, literature, business, and education. Even Christians are very slow to apply Christian categories to the issues and problems we see around us. We are content to accept the secular terms of debate—liberal versus conservative, traditional versus progressive, Republican versus Democrat, innovative versus familiar and safe.

One January after preaching in Honolulu, I went to Maui for a week of prayer and solitude in an isolated area far from the tourist route. When the week was over, I set out to find the town of Hana, a reputedly picturesque place that people told me I had to see.

I drove all over the region with a map looking for Hana. No luck. Finally I went into a general store, walked up to the woman behind the counter, and said, "I've been searching all over for Hana. Where is it?"

She looked at me—a little perturbed, I thought.

"You're standing right in the middle of Hana," she said. "This is it. There's only one store in Hana. You're here."

I thought this was a parable for all the troubles we have about praying, obeying, and finding the kingdom of God. We look for the kingdom all over the place, and we're right in the middle of it all the time.

Jesus sent the first disciples forth to proclaim, "The kingdom of God is at hand" (Matthew 10:7). For us it has come. The kingdom is here. We are followers of Jesus Christ. His grace lives in us. His work is being done wherever we are. His power is available to us.

When troubles come, it often helps to stand on the simple truth that we're right in the middle of the kingdom, just as I was right in the middle of Hana.

One time I served on a speakers' team that was introducing the ministry of healing at regional charismatic conferences. Healing is something of a controversial phenomenon. A lot of people don't believe in it. As I got up to speak, I wasn't certain myself if God would heal people that night.

I thought it was time to remind ourselves where we were. I stood up and proclaimed loudly, "The kingdom of God is at hand." I said that about six times. It was simply proclaiming what I knew to be true—that the kingdom of God was present on earth, and that signs of his kingdom would be seen that evening if we looked for them. Sure enough, many people were healed at that session. But other signs of the kingdom were visible too—in the faith of the people present, in the love and generosity of those ministering to the sick and suffering, in the delight we all took in our worship.

The kingdom of God is present in your life no matter how bad the trouble, no matter how great the suffering, no matter how bleak the prospects. You have been saved by the blood of Jesus Christ. You can call God Father. The grace of God is with you. You can stand on these truths no matter how bad it gets.

One day a physician was brought to me for healing

prayer. He was in the last stages of ALS, known as Lou Gehrig's disease—a progressive, incurable degeneration of the muscles. ALS is terrible. The man, who was still young, was completely helpless but completely conscious. He was slowly dying, and he knew exactly what was happening to him. It doesn't get much worse than ALS.

I told the man about the kingdom of God, which was present in his life despite his circumstances. God is in control, I said. He knows all about your suffering. You need never be alone, in this life or the next. The Lord will make sure that the most loving thing will be given to you. Rely on him. Surrender to his love.

All this was true for the doctor, just as it is true for you right now. These realities are stronger than anything else.

The doctor died not long after I prayed with him. After his death I received a letter from his mother that indicated that her son had changed greatly in his final days. He was freed of fear that had been plaguing him, and of the guilt that made him believe that God did not love him and that he had done something wrong to bring the disease upon himself. He died in a state of peace and joy.

We can rely on Jesus. We can confidently surrender to his love. Signs of his kingdom are all around us. We can stake our lives on these truths.

THE KINGDOM MENTALITY

We have to begin to think with a kingdom mentality and respond in terms of the kingdom, not the individual circumstances around us. This takes change—important change.

When I was a boy, people would often say, "I'm a mere mortal." Today they say, "I'm only human." We usually say this to excuse a small mistake or to deflect criticism that might come our way. It's a way of saying, "You're expecting too much of me," or, "This thing we're doing isn't very important, so don't get too upset about it."

It's true that perfection is beyond our earthly reach. It's not true that we're unimportant. In fact, we are immortal beings who will live forever, and our actions and decisions have eternal consequences for ourselves and others.

C. S. Lewis lays to rest the myth of mortality in his great essay "The Weight of Glory":

> It is a serious thing to live in a society of possible gods and goddesses, to remember that the dullest and most uninteresting person you talk to may one day be a creature which, if you saw it now, you would be strongly tempted to worship, or else a horror and a corruption such as you now meet, if at all, only in a nightmare. All day long we are, in some degree, helping each other to one or other of

these destinations. It is in the light of these over-whelming possibilities, it is with the awe and the circumspection proper to them, that we should conduct all our dealings with one another, all friendships, all loves, all play, all politics. There are no *ordinary* people. You have never talked to a mere mortal.... It is immortals whom we joke with, work with, marry, snub, and exploit—immortal horrors or everlasting splendors. [3]

Remember these words the next time you are tempted to excuse a shoddy job you've done, or to rush by acquaintances after church, or to watch television in the evening instead of spending time with your family. Every relationship is leading that other person to heaven or damnation. Life is not boring. Nothing is meaningless; nothing is indifferent.

We're human, but we're not *only* human.

If we think with a "kingdom mentality" of the kind that C. S. Lewis had, we will inevitably find ourselves out of step with the values of our culture. We will find ourselves alienated from the relentless celebration of youth and novelty that surrounds us. We're told to stay young, act young, look to the young for guidance, enjoy young people's music, wear young people's clothing styles, grow hair on bald spots, take the wrinkles out, fight sagging muscles, and be eternally attractive.

We cannot shape a successful life according to this ridiculous value system. Growing old is normal. As we grow older we acquire wisdom, which we should pass along to those younger than ourselves. Our old age is a productive time of preparation to enter eternal glory.

Thinking with a kingdom mentality can simplify many of the decisions we need to make in the course of our lives. The key question to ask is: Does this job, this relationship, this school, this amusement, take me closer to God or further away? It's not always easy to answer this question, but the question at least sets our priorities in order. And often the answer is quite clear.

I was raised on the old *Baltimore Catechism*. The first question is, "Who is God?" The second question is, "Why did God make me?" The answer says it all: "God made me to know him, and to love him, and to serve him in this world, and to be happy with him forever in the next." This is the purpose of our lives. It's not always clear how to get there, but this is the goal. Keeping the goal firmly in mind changes the way we think about everything else.

"Seeing is believing," we say. We're trained to be hardheaded, skeptical. Don't give me words and fancy theories; show me. This is the right attitude to have when we're studying science or deciding whether to buy a used car. But this is not the way to live a life of faith.

The Lord says that believing is seeing. We will never see the most important truths except through the eyes of faith. Paul writes, "We walk by faith, not by sight" (2 Corinthians 5:7). This is the literal truth. The most important values, the central commitments, are beyond sight. Our journey to know, love, and serve God is a journey in faith. Our eyes are opened by faith. Our mind is cleared by faith.

To grasp these ideas is to begin developing a kingdom mentality. These principles enable us to see the troubles of life in the right perspective; we see the forest clearly and therefore can have the right evaluation in analyzing the trouble with any particular tree. One blighted tree does not destroy a forest. One trouble does not undermine the good news of the kingdom of God.

The Power of Gratitude

We need to think with a Christian mind, but we are not simply minds. Concepts will take us only so far in times of trouble.

Gratitude will take us further. Gratitude is a very appropriate and useful virtue—perhaps *the* most important virtue. Read what one of the church fathers, Gregory of Nazianzen, said about it:

> Recognize to whom you owe the fact that you exist, that you breathe, that you understand, that you are wise, and, above all, that you know God

and hope for the kingdom of heaven and the vision of glory, now darkly and as in a mirror but then with greater fullness and purity. You have been made a son of God, coheir with Christ. Where did you get all this, and from whom?[4]

We are children of God. We are destined to live with him forever. These are the wonders in your life and mine. They are miracles. We need to treasure them and give thanks for them, as Mary did. After the birth of her Son and all the wonders surrounding it—the shepherds, the adoration of the Magi, the presentation in the temple—Luke writes that Mary "treasured all these things in her heart" (Luke 2:51).

I try to do this myself as often and as faithfully as I can. One of the most fruitful times of giving thanks occurred in 1989 when I celebrated my silver jubilee as a priest. That year was also the thirty-fifth anniversary of my experiencing God's call on my life, the thirtieth anniversary of my first vows as a Franciscan, the twentieth anniversary of being baptized in the Holy Spirit, and my fifteenth anniversary as president of the Franciscan University of Steubenville.

During some celebrations that year, I recounted my treasured memories to the students, faculty, and staff, and to my Franciscan brothers. As I did so, I recognized the power of gratitude. The words of the First Letter of Peter applied directly to me:

There is cause for rejoicing here. You may for a time have to suffer the distress of many trials; but this is so that your faith, which is more precious than the splendor of fire-tried gold, may by its genuineness lead to praise, glory, and honor when Jesus Christ appears. Although you have never seen him, you love him, and without seeing you now believe in him, and rejoice with inexpressible joy touched with glory because you are achieving faith's goal, your salvation. (1:6-9)

Here is how I express my gratitude:

I thank you, God, for all that you have done for us. I praise you for what you have given to me. Specifically I want to recount the great acts by which I have known you:

The gift of life blessed with hope;

The revelation of your kingdom as one that is victorious over all other kingdoms;

The gift of the holy men and women of old, patriarchs, prophets, judges, and martyrs;

The gift of Jesus, and mercy through his death and resurrection;

The gift of the church with apostles, prophets, pastors, teachers, evangelists;

The gift of martyrs and saints who inspire and intercede;

The holy angels, especially St. Michael and the guardian angels;

The Scriptures, God's breathed words containing the revelation of God's mysteries;

My birth into a Catholic and Christian family;

My training at a Catholic boys' school;

The gift of faith freely bestowed on the night of December 1, 1950;

The vocation to the priesthood given in February 1954;

The gift of Franciscan brothers beginning in 1957, with whom I can strive to be a faithful disciple;

The gift of Mary, the Mother of God, her apparitions, and the treasure she is in leading me to Jesus;

The gift of the priesthood in 1964, whereby I can stand in the place of Jesus, making present again his one action of salvation;

The gift of the Eucharist, the holy presence that remains with us to focus and strengthen our lives;

The gifts of baptism and confirmation, whereby I can minister to bring everlasting life and the fervor of the Holy Spirit to another person;

The gift of the sacrament of reconciliation, whereby I can pronounce God's forgiveness and welcoming into restored life and receive God's merciful forgiveness myself;

The gift of the sacrament of matrimony, whereby I can proclaim the union of two in one flesh blessed by the Lord Jesus;

The gift of the anointing of the sick, whereby I can pray officially with the power of the church for healing and for a happy death with my brothers and sisters;

The gift of healing in ordinary prayer, of prophecy, of praise, and of miracles which have filled me with awe and a sense of lowliness before God's actions;

The gift of preaching, the privilege of breaking open the word of God and feeding people with it;

The gift of teaching, the joy of instructing and forming others in the way of discipleship;

The gift of fellowship with holy men and women;

The gift of covenant, whereby those called together can build on a firm foundation and serve together;

The gift of love, whereby I can be bound in love with my Lord and then secured in love with others in good times and bad;

The gift of hope in the Holy Spirit, whereby I can believe all things, trust in all circumstances, and walk through difficulty, knowing it will end and that the end will be in the kingdom of God;

The gift of mission in the Franciscan University of Steubenville for the church, the whole body of Christ.

This prayer of gratitude has stayed with me, but is particularly powerful when celebrating anniversaries at five-year intervals, which we do as a community. Thus my thirtieth, thirty-fifth and fortieth anniversaries of ordination have been special times of overwhelming gratitude. I continue to see more deeply how everything good in my life has come from God's merciful grace.

That's what I am grateful for. That's the prayer of gratitude I pray. It strengthens me in the face of trouble.

GETTING THROUGH THE FOG

Some of our greatest sufferings involve sudden, shocking, bitter events—the medical emergency, the family crisis, the sudden death, the financial setback. But, for me at least, the worst troubles have been tough, persistent problems that settle in and don't go away. They are all-encompassing experiences that affect everything. The hardest struggles are like being lost in fog.

In the summer of 1950, I served a short tour in the merchant marine as a seaman on the freighter *Steelmaker*. My first night on board was terrifying.

We were headed at dusk up the Chesapeake River to Philadelphia Harbor. Thick fog settled over the river. As the sun went down, visibility shrank to zero. Airplanes can navigate safely in fog with their instruments. I couldn't imagine how a ship could.

The mate made my fear worse by telling me that he couldn't see well from the bridge, so I was stationed at the bow of the ship where I might have better visibility closer to water level. If I saw a ship on the starboard side, I was to ring a bell once, twice for objects to the port side, and three rings if the ship was dead ahead.

I was eighteen years old. I was a stranger on this ship. This was my first day of service and my first trip into the ocean.

As I peered into the fog, I saw all kinds of shapes. Most were imaginary, but enough were the hulls of real ships. I rang my bell furiously. I got confused. Was it one bell for starboard or one bell for port? I couldn't remember. Twice ships were dead ahead. I'm sure I rang the bell more than three times. A head-on collision wouldn't have been very good for me, standing in the bow as I was. I was thankful and exhausted when a tugboat finally came alongside and guided us to the dock.

I later learned that the survival of the *Steelmaker* didn't depend on me. The ships in the harbor were in radio contact with each other, and our pilot and mate could see everything on radar. We were not as isolated as I thought we were. I was an added precaution.

So it is with our times of deepest trouble. The fog rolls in, and we feel isolated and without recourse. We can't see our way. The shadows of what might happen are ominous. We make mistake after mistake. Final disaster seems imminent.

Later, after the fog lifts, we can see that God was in control. We can also see that we got through the time of trouble; we weren't tested beyond our endurance. But while we are walking in the fog, we can't see any of these things. God seems absent, and we are walking into situations we can't cope with.

Have you ever felt like this? Have you felt that gratitude is just a word, that thanks is impossible to give with any heartfelt meaning?

I have, and I know scores and scores of people who have felt that the tragedies of life have conquered them. The evils of life are real. Christians are not immune to them. Christians suffer the death of children, permanently disabling disease, bankruptcy, rebellion of teenage children, marital infidelity, rejection of Christianity, sexual abuse within the family, and most deeply, a sense that God has betrayed and abandoned them.

How can God allow all this and still expect me to give thanks to him? How can he allow this at all?

These are among the most difficult questions we face in our lives. Reconciling evil and the goodness of God is a pressing personal problem. It is also one of the oldest theological problems. To my mind, one of the clearest and most compelling answers is found in the Book of Job.

Job is a prosperous and much-blessed man who loses everything he has—wealth, home, sons, flocks, and finally his health. He sits on a dung hill and demands that God explain himself. God finally answers, but it is not an explanation that satisfies the intellect. He berates Job the creature for daring to question his Creator. He tells Job that he is not capable of knowing the answer to his questions or of judging God.

That satisfies Job. "Though he slay me, yet will I hope in him," (Job 13:15, NIV) he says. It's enough for Job that God reveals himself. He doesn't need answers. What he needs is God, and Job's relationship with God has been restored.

The same holds true for us. The solution to troubles—even the darkest and most severe troubles—does not lie in understanding *why* they happened. We creatures cannot unravel the mysteries of good and evil. The solution is to cling to God in hope and gratitude. He is always with us.

How do we cling to God? The answer is not a program, an insight, or an idea. It's a person—Jesus. We can cling to Jesus because he knows the most terrible troubles from the inside out. He sweated blood when he asked the Father to let the cup pass by. He was condemned on trumped-up charges, mocked by brutal soldiers and criminals, and killed in the most painful and degrading way. Just before he died he said, "My God, my God, why have you forsaken me?" (Matthew 27:46).

Here is a leader we can follow into our afflictions. We can take up our cross and follow him because he has been there before us. By faith, not by sight, we can embrace troubles as he did, knowing that this is the path of glory. When the fog closes in and we reach the edge of our endurance, we can pray to Jesus. We can act like Jesus, love like Jesus, pray like Jesus.

We can share Jesus' absolute conviction that the Father loved him and that the suffering the Father asked him to endure would bring about the salvation of the world. The Father is on our side too, loving us through trouble and suffering. Good can come out of our suffering. The Father will welcome us home after the trial and trouble have passed.

We speak of mysteries here. We do not understand the mystery of evil. We do not fully comprehend how Jesus brought about our salvation through a wicked and brutal act of execution. We do not fully understand how God can bring good out of our sufferings. But it's true, we can "count it pure joy in the midst of troubles" (see James 1:2).

One man who penetrated further into this mystery than anyone is Francis of Assisi. He asked to experience all the pain and all the love that Jesus experienced during his crucifixion. He was rewarded with the stigmata—the wounds of Christ reproduced in his feet, hands, and side.

The wounds remained with Francis until his death. They bled, they hurt, yet he cherished them. He was forever grateful to God for the privilege of sharing his Son's wounds. He was joyful. We still sing some of the many songs of praise and gratitude that Francis composed. He died united with Jesus and is remembered as one of the most Christlike men who ever lived.

Francis lived out Paul's admonition: "Sing to God with thanksgiving in your hearts. Everything you do or say, then, should be done in the name of the Lord Jesus, as you give thanks through him to God the Father" (Colossians 3:16-17).

A woman who also understood and lived out the mystery was St. Rose of Lima. She gave up everything to devote herself to a life of penance and prayer. She wrote the following entry in her diary, expressing the depths of her understanding that troubles can be God's blessing when we embrace them and allow God's grace to fill our lives:

> Our Lord and Savior lifted up his voice and said with incomparable majesty: "Let all men know that grace comes after tribulation. Let them know that without the burden of afflictions it is impossi-

ble to reach the height of grace. Let them know that the gifts of grace increase as the struggles increase. Let men take care not to stray and be deceived. This is the only true stairway to paradise, and without the cross they can find no road to climb to heaven."

When I heard these words, a strong force came upon me and seemed to place me in the middle of a street, so that I might say in a loud voice to people of every age, sex, and status: "Hear, O people; hear, O nations. I am warning you about the commandment of Christ by using words that came from his own lips: We cannot obtain grace unless we suffer afflictions. We must heap trouble upon trouble to attain a deep participation in the divine nature, the glory of the sons of God and perfect happiness of soul."

That same force strongly urged me to proclaim the beauty of divine grace. It pressed me so that my breath came slow and forced me to sweat and pant. I felt as if my soul could no longer be kept in the prison of the body, but that it had burst its chains and was free and alone and was going very swiftly through the whole world saying:

"If only mortals would learn how great it is to possess divine grace, how beautiful, how noble, how precious. How many riches it hides within itself, how many joys and delights! Without doubt they would devote all their care and concern to winning for themselves pains and afflictions. All men throughout the world would seek trouble, infirmities and torments, instead of good fortune, in order to attain the unfathomable treasure of grace. This is the reward and the final gain of patience. No one would complain about his cross or about troubles that may happen to him, if he would come to know the scales on which they are weighed when the are distributed to men."[5]

Chapter Five

—ᴧᴠᴧ—

YOU REALLY DO
HAVE AN ENEMY

Years ago, when I was in Franciscan formation at the seminary in Loretto, Pennsylvania, I became fascinated by *The Screwtape Letters* written by C. S. Lewis.

In the course of my part-time work as seminary librarian, I came across this odd book by Lewis, an Oxford literary critic who had a modest reputation as a Christian apologist. The book was a seemingly light-hearted literary fantasy. Lewis imagined that each human being has an individual devil assigned to lead him astray (the reverse of the Christian tradition that an individual guardian angel protects us). He further imagined that more experienced devils supervise the work of younger demons and tutor them in demonic techniques.

What, he asked, would the letters of a master devil to an apprentice be like? What would he tell the novice tempter about the way human beings think? What "works" from the devil's point of view? What "fails"?

My academic work at the time was very demanding: theology and philosophy with Latin texts primarily, plus a heavy regime of spiritual reading and many hours of prayer and meditation. But soon I was spending less time deciphering Latin texts and instead reading the letters of Screwtape to Wormwood.

Wormwood's job was to gain the soul of an Englishman for "Our Father Below." Screwtape's job was to guide Wormwood's work. Screwtape's amusing letters taught me as much as anything I ever read about the way the devil operates to bring trouble to our lives.

I imagined that Screwtape would show his pupil how to tempt his human in serious, spectacular sins—lust, theft, murder, and the like. Not at all. Screwtape thought pride and independence were more promising defects. He urged Wormwood to strive to make the man feel self-satisfied and complacent. Humans, he thought, were closer to the kingdom of darkness when they felt good about themselves than when they were restless and unfulfilled. The goal was to make them feel that they didn't have to serve or follow anyone, that they didn't have to be under anyone's authority, and that they didn't have much to learn.

Screwtape assured his student that an egotistical and self-satisfied human will eventually mature into a full-fledged rebel against God.

It's hard to write and talk about the role of evil spirits in our lives; harder still to sort out the specific details of demonic activity in my own life or anyone else's. The devil's work is usually very subtle, a gossamer web of Screwtape-like thoughts and desires and inclinations that exploit our defects and drain our strengths. We can stumble into evil while pursuing the good. We can be undone chasing worthy goals and taking pride in legitimate accomplishments. We can stare at the mixed motives that lie behind almost everything we do and be genuinely unable to disentangle the work of the evil one from the corruption of the world, the rebelliousness of the flesh, and the darkness of our own sinful hearts.

The devil exists; I know he does. He is at work in your life and mine. Scripture assures us that he is, and a little reflection will show you how he is at work. Yet not everything that goes wrong is caused by Satan. Seeing devils everywhere can be as great an impediment to holiness as anything else.

Satan makes use of this ambiguity as well. As Lewis points out elsewhere in his writings, the devil disguises his presence in two ways: by blinding us to his work, and by inducing us to see it everywhere.

Here I will share some things I learned about Satan's work in the lives of mature Christians. I hope to give you some tools for discernment and some weapons for the fight.

VARIATIONS ON A THEME

Satan's work in our lives can be compared to a jazz ensemble taking turns playing variations on a theme. You've probably heard it or even seen it. The group will lay down a basic theme and rhythm; then each musician will come forward and play an individual improvisation. The saxophone, drums, the clarinet, bass—all sound different and are played by musicians of different talents and temperaments. But the underlying theme is the same throughout the piece.

Most of the troubles in our lives are variations on a theme. Their particular manifestations are unique, unusual, opportunistic. But the underlying trouble is the same. The basic lie from the evil one is the same lie that the serpent whispered into the ear of Eve: God's warning doesn't really apply to you. You are special. You are a better judge than he is of what is good for you.

"You shall be like gods" (Genesis 3:5), Satan said. The first man and woman liked this idea; it was a lie, but they fell for it. When they decided to eat the forbidden fruit, they made a fateful decision to strive to be like God himself. This is the Bible's way of describing a fundamental flaw in our human natures.

Sin is a decision to put oneself above and apart from God. Our spirits are receptive to such opportunities. We like it. Every temptation is a variation on the theme, "It would be a good idea to be like God."

Our temptations usually cluster around our natural dispositions. Are you task-oriented, energetic? You'll see in yourself an inclination to impatience. Then you'll find opportunities to become angry, frustrated, and resentful.

Are you clear-sighted, realistic, practical? You may well become prone to discouragement as you plainly discern the difficult realities of life. Discouragement can become depression; depression can feed on self-pity.

Proud of your gifts and accomplishments? You find endless opportunities to be complacent, self-satisfied, disdainful of others, independent-minded.

In the 1930s, while Europe was descending into the nightmare of World War II, the *London Times* asked prominent Englishmen to answer the question, "What is wrong with the world?" The answers weren't much different from what a survey of eminent people would say today. The professors, politicians, journalists, physicians, and businessmen of the time wrote little essays pointing the finger of blame at poverty, capitalism, socialism, greed, ignorance, militarism, the arms race, fear, superstition, and all the other ills we deplore so much.

One reply stood out. It was that of G. K. Chesterton, the noted Catholic writer. To the question, "What is wrong with the world?" Chesterton responded with two words. "I am," he said.[1]

And of course he was right. If I could be the person God wants me to be, the world would be a better place. It would be better if *you* were the person God wants *you* to be. The problem with the world is that neither of us is the person God wants us to be—and neither is anyone else. If we are looking for the fundamental problem with the human race, we need to look no further than the pride in our own hearts.

I have struggled through my life with "pride of life," being proud of what I could accomplish, undertaking a challenge. This was dramatically illustrated twelve years ago when I was skiing in Colorado. I took the ski lift up to the highest mountain run. As I looked down the slope, I noticed a group of skiers going very carefully and slowly down the steep slope. I was feeling confident, and so I started down at a brisk pace. As I whisked by them, I reflected that my skiing would impress them.

I reached the group quickly, did a sharp christie and started to pass them. At that point, my right ski caught on something, and I tumbled head over heels into the snow. There I lay, covered with snow, as they slowly passed by me. Later, I reflected on the Bible proverb "Pride comes before the fall" (Proverbs 16:18). I repented, and have recalled that verse many times when I had the thought that other people would be impressed by something I was going to do.

THE HAZARDS OF WORKING FOR GOD

Screwtape and his evil assistants are especially busy when we experience spiritual renewal or become involved in significant service to others. This seems counterintuitive. A time of renewal is supposed to be an occasion when we move away from Satan's snares, not fall into them. The same is true of service. When we get involved in a ministry of service in our parish or community, we are advancing God's cause, not the devil's. Yet the advice of spiritual masters throughout the ages is clear and consistent. Times of spiritual change seem to be times to take special precautions against the enemy. The risk is that we are prone to believe that God is behind whatever lands in our minds. At a time of spiritual change, evil spiritual forces can start their work along with virtuous ones. Another stream can start flowing alongside the stream of grace, a stream that says, "I know better," or, "That's not for me," or, "I'm not like other people." This stream can muddy the pure waters of God's grace and turn our spiritual interests to destructive courses.

These attitudes can have destructive consequences when we are working together with other Christians to accomplish something for God. The primal temptation to declare "I know better" presents itself in Christian ministry as it does in any other organization involving human beings. But here normal human disagreements and differences in approach can quickly escalate into battles over who is more faithful to God. "I know better" gets expressed as "I know what God wants." Anyone who disagrees with me is thwarting the will of God himself.

If the stream that says, "I know better," is flowing strongly, we can find ourselves swiftly dismissing the spiritual ideas and commitments of other people.

"That's just an erroneous interpretation of Scripture. I don't need to believe that."

"Those people are heretics."

"That was for ignorant people two thousand years ago, recently baptized pagans. It doesn't apply to our modern culture."

"They don't respect the pope."

"That's just a teaching of the church. Human beings made it, not God."

"That's legalism."

"People who really know the Lord don't have to listen to a lot of teaching from others.

"They know from within. Doesn't Scripture say that they will no longer need men to teach them, that God himself will shepherd and teach them?"

Remember the teaching of Genesis: Adam and Eve were not born with original sin. They walked with God in the garden. They saw him face to face; they spoke with him; they knew him. Despite this incomparable gift, they were deceived and they fell. We start with original sin, darkened intellects, and weakened wills. How much easier is it for us to be wrong.

This idea should make us humble. We never need this humility more than when we are in the midst of a new and exciting spiritual experience.

SERVICE MEANS TROUBLE

The psalmist's lament, "Troubles without number surround me," (Psalm 40:12) applies especially to Christians deeply involved in ministries and service programs. The danger is especially pronounced when people get wrongly placed in leadership roles. Students of management talk about "the Peter Principle." This says simply that in an organization you rise to the level of your incompetence. In other words, if you are doing a good job in your company or business, you'll get promoted until you get a job that you can't do well.

Then you'll stay there.

The Peter Principle is painfully true. Most of us can see it at work in the large organizations we work in or otherwise come into contact with. Management consultants urge top managers to beware of the Peter Principle when they promote people to new positions.

We are especially prone to rise to the level of our incompetence when we are working in parishes, volunteer organizations, ministry projects, and other nonprofit organizations. There is always much more to do than there are people to do it. Important jobs are often available virtually for the asking. Loyalty and longevity of service tend to rank very high. Temporary changes made in an emergency can be made permanent. When we're having trouble filling a leadership slot, the faithful member who has done a good job setting up chairs can begin to look like an attractive candidate.

Misplaced executives and managers in a business organization can irritate others, waste a lot of time and money, and make it more difficult to do one's job. In a religious organization the consequences can be even more serious. Misplaced leaders breed trouble upon trouble. Defective leadership can mess up people's lives.

It can also mess up the life of the misplaced leader. Beware of getting into this position. Don't try to run away from the Lord's call to serve him and his people, but don't run ahead of it either. Be cautious about how you should use your gifts. Ask for some careful discernment. Be accountable to others for your service, and submit to regular honest evaluation. If the Lord wants to pull you up, let him do it.

SATAN IS NO INNOVATOR

Satan may play virtuoso improvisations on a basic theme in your life, but he will not do anything truly new. This can be an ironic disappointment. We all like to think we're special, that our problems are uniquely complicated or burdensome. But the temptations we undergo and the lies we entertain have all been felt and heard before. Every human being has been tempted to think that he or she is special and unique. Many millions of them have beaten back that temptation through the power of the one Man who really was unique.

We are infinitely resourceful in creating special circumstances that, in our case, justify disobeying God. They are merely improvisations on the theme Adam and Eve played in Eden when they tried to justify their misbehavior.

"Eve gave it to me. There's nothing wrong with it, but if there is, it's her fault."

"The devil made me do it."

"I didn't want to upset her. In fact, I deserve some

credit for working so hard to respect her feelings and keep peace in the household."

"Maybe it didn't work out, but it looked to us like a worthwhile broadening experience. What's wrong with that? Life is getting tough here in Eden. A little knowledge from that tree would make us better able to deal with the world effectively."

Or finally, "God, you know I love you. My heart is with you. What's the problem with a little external gesture like eating an apple?"

The devil's arguments have all been heard before. He summed up the temptations facing today's Christians in the three temptations of Christ in the desert (see Matthew 4:1-11).

"Turn those stones into bread" (4:3). In other words, if you do what you're capable of doing, there won't be any hungry people in the world anymore. Appealing, isn't it? Why aren't you out there taking care of the starving people in Bangladesh and Haiti, instead of doing all those useless spiritual things?

Then he challenged Jesus to fling himself down from the parapet of the temple and force the Father to save him (4:6). In other words, he proposed a sensational public act that would dazzle everyone. Over the years, many unique and special people have been tempted to make public display of their wonderful talents.

Finally, Satan said, "Bow down and worship me, and the world will be yours" (Matthew 4:9). In other words, let's cut a deal. Make your peace with me; accommodate my demands (which sounds so reasonable). I'll moderate my pressure on you, and together we will conquer the world.

Jesus took the harder road, made the tougher choice. It's the one we can take confidently, because he made it before us. "You shall worship only the Lord your God" (Matthew 4:10).

If you are facing a tough decision with alternatives that are hard to choose between, picture yourself in front of Jesus in the judgment. Which of the decisions would you rather defend to him as having been the right one?

THERE'S A WAR GOING ON IN YOUR HEAD

The mind is the key to the heart. Paul writes, "Take every thought captive to make it obedient to Christ" (2 Corinthians 10:5). To a large degree we grow in holiness as we gain control of that caldron of impressions, memories, dreams, ideas, and beliefs that is our thought life.

The caldron bubbles when our defenses are down. Irrational, crazy, pleasant thoughts surface at the end of a long day.

"Why don't I just take off?" you think. "Just get in the car with a few hundred dollars and my credit cards and vanish down the expressway."

You are sitting in your office after a tense meeting. "I think I'll go back there and tell them what I really think of them. In fact, why don't I just tell them all off."

You wake up in the middle of the night, frightened and weak and puny. "What am I doing here? Where am I going? Who am I?"

Where is the stuff in your head coming from? There are only three known sources for our thoughts. One: God, inspiration, the Holy Spirit. Two: ourselves and our often grumbling flesh—our hang-ups, fears, emotions, intuition, cleverness, prejudices, desires, ambitions, ideals, and dreams. Three: Satan. That's all there is.

Evil spiritual forces can influence your thought life. Here are a few things I have learned about how to get the upper hand in that struggle inside your head.

Write down Satan's "plan" for your life. By this I mean those particular areas of vulnerability that you are aware of. Put it on paper. Be specific about those defects you know about: an inclination to depression and self-pity, a weakness for alcohol or sexual fantasies, overwhelming ambition, fears of various kinds. That's where the thought battle will rage when you are anxious and distracted.

Ask the question C. S. Lewis asked when he was writing *The Screwtape Letters*: how would the devil attack you if he could do what he wanted with you? If you are inclined to depression, he will probably try to make you despair of God's love. If you are complacent, he will push you in the direction of arrogance and smugness. If you are meticulous, he will try to make you scrupulous.

If you don't think you have any character defects, ask someone who knows you well to help. The people you live and work with know you better than you think. If possible, ask a wise Christian who is close to you to regularly evaluate your progress.

SEE HOW JESUS HANDLED TEMPTATION

As part of your self-examination, study the gospel accounts of Satan's temptation of Jesus. Especially reflect on Satan's claim to be prince of this world. To Jesus he says, "Look at the kingdoms of this world, all the powers, all the nations, all the wealth. If you adore me, I will bestow it on you" (Matthew 4:8-9).

Jesus does not dispute this claim. Satan is right. He is the prince of this world until his days run out. Until Christ comes again, Satan is in charge of all those seeking first money, power, reputation, and conquest. Those who put those things first—ahead of God and obedience to his Word—come under Satan's domination. He is their prince.

Be realistic about this. We should be properly fearful of the spiritual consequences of loving the world first.

Powerful as Satan is, seductive as his kingdom may be, dangerous as his stratagems are, we can successfully resist him. He has already lost the war. He'll lose the particular battle over you if you stand up on the name, the cross, and the blood of Jesus Christ.

We're not used to the notion that a malevolent spiritual being has a plan to destroy us personally. Get used to it, but don't be intimidated by it. Satan isn't equal to Jesus. He lies crushed under Jesus' feet. He can't dominate us. He can't overcome us. With complete authority and confidence we say, "Away with you, Satan" (Matthew 4:10).

We have a sly little saying in our culture: "The devil made me do it." We say it with a little smirk, a grin—when we're caught stealing a kiss, or padding the expense account, or snatching something out of the cookie jar. "The devil made me do it." It means, "Hey, I'm really a nice person. I mean well. Don't be so strict. If anything is wrong, blame it on that creature the devil, who doesn't really exist anyway."

Well, the devil *does* exist, and we need to master him. Jesus says, "Away with you, Satan." We can stand with him and say the same thing. "Away with you, Satan, away. Jesus says, 'Go.' By the power of his cross, his name, and his blood, I say, 'Go.'"

And Satan will go. We can count on it.

Chapter Six

—ɯ—

THE HEDGE IS DOWN
—THE STRONGHOLD INVADED

Story number one begins in the 1960s.

We had built a lovely new monastery at the College of Steubenville, but we Franciscans were experiencing some problems with the yard. We didn't have much privacy. Two sides of the yard were bounded by walls of the building. One side backed up to the cliff over the Ohio River. The fourth side was open.

Wild dogs that lived in the woods came running through the yard. At night couples would wander in, hand in hand, for private talks. The priests would regularly have their privacy interrupted by curious visitors examining the monastery walls and looking for a different view of the Ohio River at the bottom of the cliff.

After a few weeks of these intrusions, the superior of the house called in the groundsmen and ordered a hedge. A few days later sturdy hedge plants bordered the fourth side of the yard, and soon they were four feet high. For twenty years the hedge preserved our privacy.

Then a new superior was appointed. He hadn't lived in the monastery when it was first built, and he was bothered at seeing the blight on the hedge leaves. He tore the hedge down. Within days a steady stream of dogs, students, and tourists began visiting our yard.

Now we have a new hedge.

Story number two reflects on a thousand years of Jewish history. The human storyteller was the cultured, lyrical, passionate Hebrew prophet Isaiah. He was speaking for God, in divinely inspired verses that have been preserved as the "Vineyard Song" in the fifth chapter of the Book of Isaiah.

My friend had a vineyard on a fertile hillside, said the prophet. He spaded it, cleared it, and planted the choicest vines. He built a hedge around it to protect it, built a watchtower, and hewed out a winepress. It was hard, dirty toil in the Palestinian sun.

Then my friend waited for the vines to bear fruit. He waited in vain. Fruit came, but it was bad fruit. In righteous wrath the owner of the vineyard tore down the hedge, opened the vineyard to marauders, and gave it to grazing.

"I will make it a wasteland," he said. "It shall not be pruned or hoed but overgrown with thorns and briers. I will command the clouds not to send rain upon it" (Isaiah 5:6).

The interpretation of this parable was clear to those whom Isaiah was addressing. The vineyard was the houses of Israel and Judah. They had persistently failed to bear fruit after centuries of careful and generous cultivation by Yahweh their Father. So God decided to tear down the hedge that was protecting the people. The land was opened to marauders. The northern kingdom of Israel fell first; then the people of Judah were carried off into exile.

When the hedge came down, God's protection was lifted—both in the monastery on the hill in Steubenville and in the land of Israel.

LIVING IN TROUBLED TIMES

The hedge around North American Christians is down.

For generations we've enjoyed some measure of protection from ideas, movements, entertainments, and pressures that would destroy our character, our families, and ultimately our faith. The protection has been spotty. Many of us have a tendency to romanticize the "good old days," when children knew their place and everyone knew the right thing to do. But an ideal world has never existed and never will in this life. Even when Christian values enjoyed the strongest public acceptance, many millions of American Christians never really enjoyed much protection, and, of course, everyone still sinned—sometimes extravagantly.

But for much of our history American Christians have enjoyed a good deal of protection from hostile forces. One of God's qualities is that he surrounds those who follow him with his protection. At the beginning of the Book of Job, Satan and God are having a discussion about why those who love God are righteous. God points to Job.

"Have you considered my servant Job?" he asks. "For there is no one on the earth like him. He is blameless and upright, fearing God and avoiding evil" (Job 1:8).

Satan scoffs. "Does Job fear God for nothing? Have you not put a hedge around his household and everything he has so that I can't get at him?" (Job 1:9-10).

So God agrees to let Satan breach the hedge. You know the rest of that magnificent story. Satan destroys everything Job has. He loses his children, his wealth, his household, his reputation, and his health. He laments; he wails; he demands an explanation from God. But he never loses faith in God, and he ultimately bows in submission when God reveals himself.

The story is a parable for us. We've had a hedge of protection around us. But now it has been breached, and we're facing trials we've never faced before.

Historically speaking, this is not a new situation for Christians. In fact, many millions of Christians in the world today face far greater problems in their societies than we face. But it's a new situation for most of us. The generation that grew up in the 1950s and early 1960s grew up behind the hedge. We were fairly certain that anything that would be a serious threat to our moral character and Christian ethic would be labeled that way. The Legion of Decency categorized movies. The bishops and pastors did not hesitate to speak out about dangerous ideas and risky entertainment. Standards of sexual behavior were known, if not always followed.

When I was young, one of the great movie controversies raged around one line of dialogue in *Gone with the Wind*. At the end of the movie, after being abused and lied to and exploited by Scarlett O'Hara for two-and-a-half hours, Rhett Butler decides to leave her. She wails, "What's going to happen to me?" He answers, "Frankly my dear, I don't give a damn."

Some religious leaders thought this type of language was totally inappropriate and they condemned the movie as unfit for good people. Others disagreed.

That controversy seems comical now, but it shows the kind of protection people had if they wanted to use it. Sinful things were labeled pretty clearly. The hedge around the church simplified a lot of decisions.

The hedge is down now. Some remnants of it are still standing. And many Christians don't need a hedge in order to raise their children well. But marauders are tramping through the land. The stronghold has been invaded. Confusion swirls over many once-settled issues. To learn how to deal with the trouble in our lives, we have to learn how to deal with these marauders.

The problem is not so much wrongdoing as confusion about wrongdoing among people who shouldn't be confused. Some Christians have abandoned God's way and God's morality. Many other Christians see people sinning and they aren't worried about it anymore. They aren't shocked. Many who claim to be Christians today condone violations of the commandments. They try to look at the bright side of family breakdown. They tolerate pornography. They excuse shameless, prodigal greed. They look benignly on exploitation of the poor and ignorant. These people do all this and worship God too.

An atmosphere of easygoing tolerance pervades society and the church. Many Christians are weak in their judgments because no one else seems concerned. It's hard to fight a lonely battle; it's easier to think that something is wrong with you when no one else seems upset about matters that trouble you. It's easier to go with the flow—to rock with the rest of the swingers on Saturday night and go to church on Sunday, "if that's your thing."

We're sure our civilization is progressive and advanced, but morally our condition is the same as that of Israel under King Ahab and Queen Jezebel about twenty-six hundred years ago. Jezebel introduced pagan fertility gods into Israel. The king let her do it, and soon the people of Israel were worshipping Canaanite fertility deities along with Yahweh (1 Kings 16:31-33).

The explanation went something like this: "Yahweh is a good God, but he's mainly a God of the hills, good for nomads and wandering in the desert. Now that we're a settled people, we need to honor the gods that are in charge of the crops."

The Israelites made a disastrous mistake. Yahweh turned out to be a jealous God. When the people had sunk too deeply into sin, he destroyed the kingdom of Israel, then Judah. The people went into exile, never to return to their former glory.

We are in the same situation today. A crude paganism dominates the day-to-day life of our people. An antireligious ideology controls the opinions of the culture-forming elites. And Christians are exceedingly reluctant to confront the situation as it really exists.

Opponents—Nice and Not So Nice

What sorts of people are opposing us? For the most part they are nice people. They aren't calling for Christians and Jews to be rounded up and killed. They aren't obviously fanatics. They dress well, speak well, and appear to mean well—at least most of the time. In the West they are mostly people who identify themselves as humanists in some way. Christian humanism has a long and glorious history. In fact, Judeo-Christian religion provides the only solid basis for humanism. But the people who oppose us call themselves "secular" humanists or simply "secular" people. They seek to establish human value and dignity apart from God.

Secular humanists hold that supernatural religion is not only irrelevant but harmful. They reject the biblical view of man as a gravely flawed creature in need of repentance and salvation. The best thing men and women can do to advance human welfare, they say, is to renounce the notion that God will save us. Our fate is in our own hands. Progress comes from our own resources and creativity. Christians and Jews who operate from a belief in eternal life and who believe in the biblical analysis of human problems are free to practice their faith in private. They should not be free to work to make these views part of public policy.

The antireligionists are especially interested in sexual behavior, both as a key area of "freedom" and as a symbolic area where religious views have been especially influential. Their basic view is that no sexual behavior between consenting adults should be prohibited. In fact, giving free rein to one's sexual urges is viewed as a positive good. Rules on sex are bad. Thus we have virtually no legal or social sanctions against premarital or extramarital sex, homosexual or bisexual behavior, divorce, or other sexual practices once frowned upon. Abortion on demand was legalized in the United States in 1973 as part of its drive for maximum personal freedom.

The church also faces opposition from Marxists and radical Muslims. Secular humanists, Marxists, and radical Muslims do not work together. Neither do they always operate from a well-defined program of hostility to Christians. The number of people who are influenced by these groups is much larger than the number of self-declared enemies of the church. Yet the conflict is there, and it is continuing.

We are doing poorly in this conflict. Radical Islam, a very simple religion with a very broad appeal, is growing at a rapid rate. Marxism may have lost its luster as an ideology, but the Marxist ideal of a perfect, godless utopia on earth remains the political fantasy of socialists, anarchists, and revolutionaries the world over.

In the West the glitter of the boundless abundance of capitalist materialism has bewitched us. The hedge has come down, and in come…consumer electronics, fancy cars, executive jets and yachts, summer homes, luxury food, imported liquor and silk neckties, gold and diamonds, fancy furs, and a DVD player in every room of the house.

We are preoccupied with making money. We idolize the men and women who make a lot of it. We are caught up in a terrible drive to acquire more, to have the most, to enjoy the best—and to brag about what we have. We must break with this materialism which is now the mainstream of American life. Oppressive love of money and of the things money can buy is the very air we breathe, the atmosphere in which we raise our families, educate our children, and worship our God.

The hedge comes down, and we are overwhelmed with…toys—toys that expose us to people living every indulgent lifestyle, every lie, every fantasy of the flesh. Television is the center of the American home. Except for homes where people watch their own TVs individually in their own rooms, the television is the very center of domestic life, often established as the centerpiece of a room called the "home entertainment center." An archaeologist of the future studying the living habits of American families would immediately identify the television as the household god, the holy thing around which life revolves.

There are some excellent programs on television; there are some atrocious programs. The problem is that the average American watches between thirty and forty hours of television a week. We worship on Sunday, maybe read a little Scripture some other days. But we watch television for as many hours as we work at paying jobs.

The hedge comes down, and in comes...confusion. How do we evaluate our condition? Yes, television is offensive, and abortion is a horror, and the poor are neglected, and young people are leaving the church by the millions. But the economy is strong. The stock market is okay. Our political system is stronger than the ones in Mexico and Bolivia. And we're good people.

The hedge is down...and Satan moves at will in places where the church once stood strong.

POWER TO PERSEVERE

But there is another side to the picture. The hedge is down...but this is also the time of the greatest growth of Christianity in history. The number of Christians in Africa has grown from 10 million in 1900 to 360 million in 2000. There are 2 billion Christians in the world today. By 2025 that number will increase to 2.6 billion, with most of them living in Africa, Asia, and Latin America. Much of this increase has come through the growth of Pentecostal Christianity, with its emphasis on healing, spiritual gifts, miracles, and evangelism. By 2050 there will be 1 billion Pentecostal Christians in the world.

This is an awesome outpouring of spiritual power.

A decisive choice lies before us. We don't have to flee in terror before the corruption and confusion and godlessness of the marauders who've breached the hedge. God's renewal provides an alternative. His power is ours for the asking. We can be confident and effective, saying, "Lord, just show me what you want me to do, and I will do it."

The Book of Revelation contains a warning that should get our attention. In the early chapters of the book, the Lord demands that various churches change their ways or be judged harshly. One of these churches is the church in Laodicea, and it sounds very much like the church in North America. The Lord condemns the complacent Laodiceans: "I know your works; you are neither cold nor hot. I wish that you were either cold or hot. So, because you are lukewarm, and neither cold nor hot, I am about to spit you out of my mouth" (Revelation 3:15-16, NRSV).

The Laodiceans' wealth has blinded them to their real spiritual condition: "For you say, 'I am rich, I have prospered, and I need nothing.' You do not realize that you are wretched, pitiable, poor, blind, and naked" (Revelation 3:17, NRSV).

The Lord is issuing this harsh warning to committed Christians who knew the love of God and the power of the Spirit, who knew what it meant to make a break with the surrounding paganism and take a new path. They are people who should have known better. To them he says, "You do not realize that you are wretched, pitiable, poor, blind, and naked."

With the hedge down we can see in sharper relief what is a blessing in our life and what isn't. What is good is what God has blessed us with: salvation, grace, brothers and sisters, forgiveness of sins, the church, a mission. We can spend our days and nights in the glittering fairyland of American society and know deep down that it is God's blessings that count. We are going to be held accountable for these blessings at the last judgment. You, me, your spouse, your children, your pastor and friends—all of us are going to stand before the whole creation at the end of time and be judged for what we did with what God gave us. Did we bury the talent in the ground, or did we put it to work?

If we know this deep down, then we know we are wretched, pitiable, poor, blind, and naked. We are afflicted with a basic inclination to sin, a basic weakness, a basic vulnerability. We might drive a nice car, live in a nice house, and have plenty of money in the bank, and still cry out to the Lord every morning, "Don't allow me to be tempted beyond my strength, because I will betray you."

If we know God's power, we know we are wretched. If we live in his strength, we know we are pitiable. If we are going to do his work, we know we are blind and naked. Our very life is drawn from him. Our identity and our power, our work and our competence, our vision and our strength—all these are blessings from God that we have done nothing to deserve.

Offering advice to the Laodiceans, the Lord continues: "Buy from me gold refined by fire so that you may be rich" (Revelation 3:18, NRSV).

The gold is God's grace. Just ask, he is saying. Just ask. I have what you need. My kingdom is the only one worth living in. My kingdom is the only one whose values you want. Come to me, and I will give it to you. Stay out there, and I will spit you out of my mouth.

These are rough words to people who call themselves Christians. Why are you talking to us like that, Lord? Why don't you rebuke the pagans next door, the enemies down the street?

Because you are all I have, the Lord says. You said you would follow me and serve me, and the future of the church and the world lies with you. And you compromise. You hold back because of fear of what your neighbors might say. You wander off to follow the glitter of money and success and material accumulation. You take it easy while my church burns.

TAKE HEED

It's hard to talk this way, but I am trying to see the state of the church and the world as the Lord might see it. It's hard to discern what our response should be to this rather bleak prospect. The task looks intimidating; and it is. We may be all the Lord has, and it is easy to think that we aren't nearly enough.

We aren't. That's the first part of our response: to realize that whatever we are called to do is only part of what the Lord is doing. We have a role to play in the restoration of his kingdom, but only one role. He is moving among other people and in ways that we are not aware of.

The second aspect of our response repeats something I've been saying every time I get a chance. I've said it before in this book, and I'll say it again. Seek the Lord for the answers and the grace. We do not have the answers. We certainly do not have the strength, the courage, and the wisdom to effectively counter our foes by ourselves. Apart from God we can do nothing.

The third response is to be a people of warning. Our society has gotten very comfortable with the toys and entertainment of the consumer culture. Someone has to tell people that the hedge is down. We live today in a society of warnings. Tobacco causes cancer, heart disease, and emphysema; alcohol with some prescription drugs can kill you; laboratory rats have died eating several pounds of the sweetener in diet soft drinks. Product liability is a booming specialty in the legal profession. The old English common-law tradition of *caveat emptor*, let the buyer beware, is a thing of the past.

People today need to hear that something in their homes is far more dangerous to them than tobacco, alcohol, and tainted food. It threatens their eternal salvation. There's no protection anymore. Television, movies, magazines, education, music—all are being contaminated with a vision of life that leads us away from God. Not everything we find there is bad. But the hedge is down and the battle is on. We need the vigilance of people who know the battle is within our ranks.

During World War II, the constant refrain given by every vendor who didn't have a commodity in stock and every service manager who didn't provide an advertised service was, "You know, there is a war on." There is a war on today. We also need to know that our war ends in victory for the kingdom of God, as certainly as World War II ended on V.J. Day, the Feast of the Assumption of Mary, August 15, 1945.

Chapter Seven

—⚏—

WALKING IN FAITH AND DISCERNING GOD'S WILL

The psychology department at the Franciscan University of Steubenville offers a popular course that deals with trust. The course includes a very interesting laboratory workshop to help students understand how difficult it can be to truly trust. Each student is blindfolded and led by another student on a tour of the campus. They go up and down hills, through ditches, along the cliff over the Ohio River, through crowds of people in the dining hall, into the student center, up to one of the classroom buildings. The students have an inner experience of the truth of a verse in 2 Corinthians: "We walk by faith and not by sight" (5:7).

Most of the students experience the inner terror that walking by faith breeds. It's frightening suddenly to be deprived of your sight. It can be terrifying to find yourself required to rely on the good sense and intelligence of another person—usually someone you've harbored private doubts about.

It can be disturbing to walk by faith. It can also look foolish to others.

In the summer of 1957, I was an officer stationed at Andrews Air Force Base. I had decided that God was calling me to be a priest in the Franciscan Third Order Regular. I made a novena to Our Lady of Perpetual Help. I went to novena services weekly for eight months. I believed that Our Lady was leading me and making this vocation possible.

The problem was that I had nine more months on my commitment to the Air Force. I applied for an early release to go to the seminary. My superior officer and the general in charge of the Eastern Defense Command turned down my request. I said to my assistant, "I guess God doesn't want me this year."

He replied, "But you told me you believed our Lady was opening the doors for you to join the Franciscans this September. If you believe it, appeal to the Chief of Chaplains."

So, I made an appointment with the Acting Chief of Chaplains at the Pentagon. I prayed hard and that office recommended a reversal of the decision. For two months, I waited for action and nothing happened. The seminary informed me that I must report by the first Sunday in September or wait another year. The Air Force informed me that I must receive my discharge by the preceding Tuesday or they could not process me out in time to report to the seminary.

I asked my friends to pray and I waited. Then the final Tuesday came. Nothing happened. At 4:00 P.M. the offices closed. As my friends walked by the office, they said such things as "Tough luck, Mike," or "Nice try," and "Well, we will be together for another year."

I kept praying to Our Lord, focusing on the intercession of Our Lady of Perpetual Help. Actually, my prayer was more like "but you promised!"

I sat alone in the building, and at approximately 5:00 P.M. a sergeant came to my door. He said, "Are you Lieutenant Scanlan?"

I nodded and he said, "I don't understand it, but we just received this on our wire reserved for top security communications."

I read the message. It said I was discharged effective immediately.

That weekend I reported to the Franciscans, and I have been grateful every day since then. I also have more faith.

I walk by faith and not by sight in the big things too. One spring, as I watched the blindfolded students from the psychology class being led around the campus, I reflected on the trust I had to place in the pastoral authorities God has put in my life. I have a spiritual director, religious superiors to whom I owe obedience, the local bishop, and the pope. My life is in their hands. I need to trust them. Of course, I need first to trust God, whom I believe called me into this life to live under their authority. Indeed, I had better walk by faith, or I'll never live what I have publicly professed to be my life.

FAITH ISN'T SIGHT

We walk by faith, not by sight.

The first thing to understand is that we walk. We are placed here on this earth to do things. Even if Adam and Eve had not sinned, there probably would have been plenty for them to do in paradise. Since they did sin, there's far more work to do to preach the gospel and to restore the kingdom of God than we can even imagine.

What work has God given you to do?

A lot of the troubles in our lives stem from bad answers to this question, unclear answers, or no answers at all. We get in touch with the Lord, and then we find ourselves doing—what? In many cases, we do the first or second thing that comes along. After a few years of this we are frustrated, bitter, and upset.

After talking to literally thousands of people over the years about their failures and frustrations in serving the Lord, I have developed a series of questions that I think are basic to discerning your walk in faith. This is what I ask.

What are you called to do?

How are you positioned?

How are you equipped?

They are simple questions, basic questions. But answering them is seldom easy, and sometimes it is quite complex.

As you attempt to answer them, it's important to understand that we're talking about a radical break with the ordinary way of doing things. The basic Scripture that I use as a foundation for this discernment is Romans 12. Paul writes: "Do not conform any longer to the pattern of this world, but be transformed by the renewal of your mind. Then you will be able to test and approve what God's will is, his good, pleasing, perfect will" (12:2).

Paul is writing to committed Christians. The Romans knew the Lord Jesus; they knew the power of the Holy Spirit; they were already living a form of Christian community. To people like this—people very much like you and me—he says, be transformed. Don't settle for ordinary organizational patterns, the old boy network that's the familiar way of getting things done. Be transformed by the renewing of your mind. The mind is the last element of the human personality to change. The heart changes, the will changes, emotions change—lots of things change before your mind does. Finally you change the way you think: how you view the world, your opinions, your approach to life.

"Then you will be able to attest what God's will is, his good, pleasing, and perfect will" (Romans 12:2b). Here is a promise. When we allow the Spirit to transform our minds, then we are positioned to receive his blessings. When our mind is renewed, we will see God's will for us. Then we can ask the three questions.

GOD CALLS

First question: what is your call? We treat much of the work of the kingdom of God as part-time, volunteer work that we get into by signing up in the back of church. But Jesus didn't ask for volunteers. He *called* people.

"As Jesus was walking beside the Sea of Galilee, he saw two brothers, Simon now called Peter and his brother Andrew, and they were casting their nets into the sea, for they were fishermen. 'Come, follow me,' Jesus said, 'and I will make you fishers of men.' At once they left their nets and followed" (Matthew 4:18-20).

Another passage: "As Jesus was passing by, he saw a man named Matthew sitting at the tax collector's booth. 'Follow me,' he told him, and Matthew got up and followed him" (Matthew 9:9).

You've heard and read these passages hundreds of times. Notice how different Jesus' way of getting people into a new job is from the ordinary human way. Most of the time we get into positions because of economic need, greed, ambition, flattery, boredom, or simple convenience. In church work the motive is usually pressure. We wind up doing jobs because someone asked us to, or because there was no one else and people were absolutely desperate. Consequently, a lot of people in church work are in the wrong position.

By contrast, the Lord Jesus calls. He says, be my disciple, be formed by me, learn from me, think like I think, act like I act. This conviction that God has called you is the basis for your walk in faith. With it you will trust the Lord: you will trust that he will provide for you, and you will have confidence to go to him for what you need to do the job he has given you.

When I was studying theology in the seminary, I was excited about being a missionary in Brazil. I joined our mission club and became president. I led mission support activities and corresponded regularly with our Franciscan missionaries in the Amazon district of Brazil.

They in turn requested the Minister Provincial to assign me to their missions once I was ordained a priest.

Two days before my ordination, I met with the Provincial and he informed me that he was assigning me to be acting academic dean at the College of Steubenville. I was confused and sad, but I knew it was God's will.

I took academic administration studies at Catholic University during the summer, and I reported to Steubenville. I grew excited and fulfilled with the ministry at the College. I no longer thought of the missions. Seven years later I was asked to give a retreat in the Amazon missions. I looked forward to it, but when I visited all the missions, I knew I didn't belong there. The missionary work I had imagined was much different than the actual work in the missions. I thanked God for the call of obedience that sent me to Steubenville.

How do you determine your call? It can happen in many ways, in many different chronologies. Almost always, it takes some time.

You need to hear it. Somewhere along the line you should hear God say that such and such a course is his will. For the very biggest decisions—marriage, priesthood, religious life—you need to have a clear understanding of God's call before you take the final step. You say the vows after you know it is his will.

How do you hear it? Either by yourself or through another. Over the years you learn to hear God through prayer and reading Scripture. You learn how God speaks and the ways he speaks. I have found a prayer journal especially helpful.

You can also hear God through other people. When you are facing important decisions, talk them over with a mature Christian who knows you well, who knows how to listen to God, and who believes he or she has heard something for you from God.

Even that is only the beginning. If you hear a call through another person, you have to confirm it yourself in prayer.

The call has to be tested—first against God's Word in Scripture, against the teaching of the church, against tradition. Then you have to submit it to others—primarily those who share your life. The circumstances have to agree with the call. There has to be a fit. God has to open the doors; practical details like finances have to be settled.

It's not uncommon to hear God's call correctly but to get the timing wrong. Often God will prepare you for a future work by putting a desire to do it in your heart years before it's time. I knew of a couple who heard a call to be missionaries in Uganda. They knew they had heard God; several people confirmed it. So they packed up and caught the next plane to Uganda and said, "Here we are." The Ugandan Christians were very surprised to see them; they hadn't heard the same call these Americans had. So the Americans stayed in Uganda until their money ran out, and then they went home.

Two years later their church decided to sponsor a missionary effort in Uganda and asked for volunteers to go. The circumstances were finally right for them to act on the call they had heard from God years earlier.

The call is the foundation, the basis for a walk in faith. Without the call you won't have the faith that must sustain you when sight doesn't work anymore.

BEING IN THE RIGHT SPOT

How are you positioned? That's the second question. Are you in the right place in the body of Christ to do what you think you should be doing?

This raises a series of questions that many people find boring and troublesome. It opens up a branch of theology called ecclesiology. Where do you fit in the body of Christ? Are you related properly to your pastor? to your bishop? to the Holy Father and authorities in Rome? Is the ministry constituted in the right way?

The Holy Spirit works through constituted authority. In fact, one of the great currents of renewal is the rediscovery of a variety of gifts and roles and ministries, all functioning in unity, as the body of Christ, because they are properly related to the whole through authority.

The documents of Vatican II have some useful direction in this area.

First, the council unequivocally affirms the validity of the charisms of the laity. It says, "Though they differ from one another in essence and not only in degree, the common priesthood of the faithful and the ministerial or hierarchical priesthood are none the less interrelated."[1] Furthermore, the council clearly states that the gifts we have are for the benefit of the church as a whole:

> It is not only through the sacraments and Church ministries that the same Holy Spirit sanctifies and leads the People of God and enriches it with virtues. Allotting his gifts "to everyone according as he will" (1 Corinthians 12:11), he distributes special graces among the faithful of every rank.[2]

What are these graces for?

> By these gifts he makes them fit and ready to undertake the various tasks or offices advantageous for the renewal and upbuilding of the church, according to the words of the apostle: "the manifestation of the Spirit is given to everyone for profit" (1 Corinthians 12:7). These charismatic gifts, whether they be the most outstanding or the more simple and widely diffused, are to be received with thanksgiving and consolation, for

they are exceedingly suitable and useful for the needs of the church.[3]

The glue that holds all this ministry together is authority. Real authority was given by the Lord to Peter and to his successors on the chair of Peter. We need to be properly related to this authority. We can float. We can do our own thing, set things up for our own convenience, not bother ourselves with the difficulties of getting positioned properly. But there will be a price for such neglect. The fruit of the work will be stunted. And you will have few allies when the inevitable trouble comes.

THE RIGHT TOOLS

How are you equipped?

This is the third question. You've been called to do something; the call is confirmed by the timing, the circumstances, and the agreement of your pastor, spouse, and trusted friends. You're positioned correctly. The ministry is set up properly, and the correct authorities support it. Now, do you have what it takes to do what you're supposed to do? John Paul II put it well in his apostolic exhortation *Christifidelis Laici*:

> The Holy Spirit, while bestowing diverse ministries in Church communion, enriches it still further with particular gifts or prompting of grace,

called *charisms*. These can take a great variety of forms both as a manifestation of the absolute freedom of the Spirit who abundantly supplies them, and as a response to the varied needs of the Church in history. The description and the classification given to these gifts in the New Testament are an indication of their rich variety. "To each is given the manifestation of the Spirit for the common good. To one is given through the Spirit the utterance of wisdom, and to another the utterance of knowledge according to the same Spirit, to another faith by the same Spirit, to another gifts of healing by the one Spirit, to another the working of miracles, to another prophecy, to another the ability to distinguish between spirits, to another various kinds of tongues, to another the interpretation of tongues" (1 Corinthians 12:7-10; cf. 1 Corinthians 12:4-6, 28-31; Romans 12:6-8; 1 Peter 4:10-11).[4]

Whether they be exceptional and great or simple and ordinary, the charisms are *graces of the Holy Spirit that have*, directly or indirectly, *a usefulness for the ecclesial community*, ordered as they are to the building up of the church, to the well-being of humanity, and to the needs of the world.

Today we see an abundance of charisms among lay people. In referring to the apostolate of the lay faithful, the Second Vatican Council writes:

For the exercise of this apostolate, the Holy Spirit who sanctifies the People of God through the ministry and the sacraments gives to the faithful special gifts as well (cf. 1 Corinthians 12:7), "allotting to everyone according as he will" (1 Corinthians 12:11). Thus may the individual, "according to the gift that each has received, administer it to one another" and become "good stewards of the manifold grace of God" (1 Peter 4:10), and build up thereby the whole body in charity (cf. Ephesians 4:16).[5]

If you are not equipped for the service you are in, you should get equipped. If you don't have the training for the work, get it. If power is lacking in your service, beseech the Lord for it. If you don't have adequate leadership, figure out how you are going to get it from somewhere else. These are tough questions, hard issues. They are the issues that keep us up nights praying and pondering. It often takes humility to get the right leadership in place, admission of mistakes to get a group equipped to do the job the Lord wants it to do.

But it needs to be done—courageously and fearlessly. We have the immense task of renewing the church and evangelizing the world. This is something that must be done with renewed minds and renewed hearts. We need God's plan, not our own. So let's hear our call, get positioned correctly, and get equipped rightly—and the Lord's fruit will be borne in our work.

The walk in faith is long and hard. Times will come when we will look foolish to others and appear foolish even to ourselves. You've read the passages in Scripture about trouble. Here is a warning you probably haven't read. It's from St. Polycarp's letter to the Philippians:

> Prepare yourselves for the struggle, serve the Lord in fear and truth. Put aside empty talk and popular errors; your faith must be in him who raised our Lord Jesus Christ from the dead and gave him a share in his own glory and a seat at his right hand.[6]

WARNINGS AND WEAPONS

Here are some attitudes and warnings—some weapons, if you will—for the faith walk when the going gets tough.

Guard Your Heart. Renewal and transformation may be primarily a matter of renewing the mind, but walking by faith is a matter of the heart. The heart is the key; I guarantee it will be attacked.

I have known scores, hundreds of people who've been troubled by a faith crisis. A genuine faith crisis isn't silly, but lots of less serious upheavals masquerade as faith crises. In the seminary we did a lot of fasting. Men would suddenly have a faith crisis over whether fasting was really right because Jesus was now risen from the dead. It became a big issue. There was only one problem: they always had those crises on fast days, never on days when we were eating normally.

Many so-called "faith crises" are brought on by problems with sex. The college kid in a bad sexual relationship, the married person embroiled in an affair, the priest struggling with celibacy—all of these troubles may manifest themselves as a struggle with faith.

The battering you take as you walk by faith may sometimes shake that faith. It's very important to separate the troubles of your walk from a fundamental faith crisis. You may get lonely, confused, and tired, and wish to God that he would give you a respite from your struggles with sin and temptation. You can be having a terrible time and still be firm in your faith. You can still know that Christ is the Son of God, that Jesus is reigning at the right hand of the Father, that the gospel is true, and that the Bible tells us how to live. You can believe all this, know that your faith is based on facts, know that you can trust the Catholic church, and still be in inner turmoil.

Troubles will come, but they won't involve your faith *unless* you let them. The attack will threaten your energy, conviction, and commitment. The crises in your life will probably come because of the world, the flesh, and the devil—not because of theological doubts about the real presence, or substitutionary atonement, or the Nicene Creed.

The faith walk is a walk with others. Life with God is a life of relationships. Guard your heart especially as it involves your relationships with other people.

Watch Out for Anger. I don't mean the flare-ups that happen in our work and day-to-day life, that come and are quickly gone. I mean anger that is nurtured and nursed, gnawed at in the depths of our hearts like a bone in a dog's mouth; anger that settles into resentment and bitterness; anger that makes a heart as hard as granite—virtually impossible to break through.

A Critical Spirit. Watch out for a critical spirit in your relationships with the people you are working with, especially if you are in a position of leadership. Few things are more demoralizing than a team member or leader who does not have confidence in his or her colleagues. Few things do more to build healthy morale than someone who fights for his or her colleagues when they're attacked, who expresses hope and confidence at every opportunity, who intercedes for them.

Pray for People You Work With. No matter how hard they are to deal with and no matter how many problems they have, you won't grow bitter about them if you are praying for them.

Where your treasure is, there your heart will be. Where your heart is, there is your walk in faith. Walk in faith, not by sight. Place your heart on the things you know—your call, your vision, the facts of your salvation. Your treasure is the Lord: "Seek the Lord and you will live" (Amos 5:4). Seek the Lord and you will find true life and true vitality.

Get rid of the mistaken notion that faith is a pious sentiment or a worldly perspective. It is the power of victory, and when we walk by true faith we are indeed victorious.

"Everyone begotten by God conquers the world and the power that has conquered the world is this faith of ours" (1 John 5:4). We have God's Word on it.

Chapter Eight

—⁓—

YOU CAN REJOICE
IN TROUBLE

Emotions are hard to understand. They trip us up. The mind penetrates them only with difficulty.

One of the murkiest emotions is joy. Consider this short verse in the fourth chapter of Philippians: "Rejoice in the Lord always! I say it again. Rejoice!" (4:4). It's a clear, simple exhortation, yet we're inclined to think it means just about anything other than what it plainly does mean.

I used to puzzle over this verse, and over other passages having to do with joy.

One day the disciples returned to Jesus after going on a successful demon-smashing expedition around the

Sea of Galilee. "Lord, even the demons submit to us in your name," they announced (Luke 10:17). Imagine their excitement. Imagine the good they had done. The whole area had been under demonic bondage. Now a bunch of fishermen and craftsmen had shown up, ordered Satan out "in the name of Jesus," and boom— the spirits were gone. Jesus listened to all this and then said, "Do not rejoice that the spirits submit to you, but rejoice that your names are written in heaven" (10:20).

Then there is this passage at the beginning of the Letter of James: "Whenever you face trials of any kind, consider it nothing but joy" (1:2, NRSV).

Why? How is this possible?

Joy crops up continually in the New Testament.

In 1 Thessalonians 5:16-17, Paul tells us: "Rejoice always, never cease praying, give thanks in all circumstances."

Trials will come upon you. In fact, if you have been seriously trying to serve the Lord, severe trials are probably already plaguing you. Chances are you've encountered some serious obstacle to your personal growth in holiness—an addiction, some disordered emotions, a pattern of sin. You can bear up under these trials with joy. "Rejoice always" is literally true.

Misconceptions about Emotions

First, a few words on ways emotions trip us up.

One mistake some Christians make is to act as if they don't have any emotions. I call it Christian stoicism. Classical stoicism says that people can avoid the pain of life by turning off the emotions. Stoicism is often presented as the ideal in religions that are cultic or pagan by nature. The Buddhist ideal, for example, is basically a stoic meditation on the essential unity of all creation. Hindu meditation is stoic. Much abuse of drugs in our own society is a conscious or unconscious effort to escape the pain of emotions, to flee into a stoic world.

Stoicism crops up in Christianity, too. There has been a would-be stoic in every class of seminarians I have ever pastored. This is the young man who gets preoccupied with penances and fasting and abject humility. Sometimes there are several stoics in a class, so you get the ridiculous situation of a couple of brothers regularly rivaling and priding themselves at being in the last place and having the dirtiest job.

The other extreme is excessive attention to emotions. Back in the 1960s "sensitivity" theorists advanced the notion that emotions were the center of life, and that it was terribly important for everyone to be keenly aware of everybody's feelings at all times. Some theorists of the sensitivity movement had proposed that to be fully human you have to fully express your feelings on all occasions, and even that you should judge everything by your feelings. Few people go to such extremes today, but echoes of sentimentality persist.

Another misconception is to equate virtue with various emotions. In particular, the virtue of humility is equated with feelings of worthlessness. This is the mistake made by the person who always feels bad about himself or herself, who is always asking for forgiveness, always repenting, always saying things that are patently untrue—such as "I am nothing and you have all these gifts," or "You are so much better than I am."

A version of this problem is manifested by the person who is always insisting that we need to have more faith. The response to every difficulty is an exhortation to have faith, to redouble our prayers for faith, and so on and so on. Real faith may lie behind this chatter, but this is not faith. Such a response often stems from anxiety or fear rather than real faith.

Our ideal is to be emotionally expressive in a way that supports our way of life. St. Augustine wrote that a Christian has emotions because we share in the life of Jesus Christ. Just as Jesus was fully human, so are we. Look at what the Gospels tell us about Jesus' emotional life.

In Mark 1 we read that Jesus was "moved with pity" at the sight of the leper (1:41). In Luke 19 we read that Jesus wept over Jerusalem because he foresaw its destruction (19:41). When Jesus sat down with the disciples at the Last Supper, he said that he had "longed" to eat this supper with them. He was filled with anger at the sight of the money changers in the temple. In the garden of Gethsemane he was filled with fear.

Jesus shows us the range of emotions—pity, sorrow, desire, longing, anger, fear, and joy. We are to have a range of emotions too. Our emotions are part of being human, and emotional expression is part of an authentic human response.

REJOICE ALWAYS?

Joy is a response to something good. It involves our emotions. It often involves our actions. In the parable the woman who found the lost coin called in the neighborhood to have a party (Luke 15:8-9). The father of the prodigal son threw a party to celebrate his son's return. Repentance is a good thing, calling for rejoicing. "There will likewise be more joy in heaven over one repentant sinner than over ninety-nine righteous people who have no need to repent," our Lord says (Luke 15:7).

Because joy is a response to something good, James writes, "Consider it pure joy, my brothers, whenever you face trials of every kind" (1:2). How is this possible? Do we like trials? No. We are joyful over trials in the same way we are joyful over repentance. Trials mean that our faith is being tested, and that means we will grow stronger, more mature, more capable, more like Christ. It is not wishful thinking or anxious chatter to say that we should be joyful in the midst of troubles. It is literally true that troubles make us stronger. Troubles reveal our weaknesses and make us rely more on the Lord. They call forth our strengths; they allow us to put our gifts to good use in the service of others.

Think of the times when you felt closest to the Lord. Probably there were times of trouble and testing when you suddenly became painfully aware of how much you need God. Consider the testimony of St. Paul:

> We do not want you to be unaware, brothers and sisters, of the affliction we experienced in Asia; for we were so utterly, unbearably crushed that we despaired of life itself. Indeed, we felt that we had received the sentence of death so that we would rely not on ourselves but on God who raises the dead. (2 Corinthians 1:8-9, NRSV)

Think of the times when you felt farthest from God, when prayer was most difficult, when your work seemed least fruitful. Often you can look back on these times and see that they were periods of great spiritual growth.

There's another reason why you can be joyful in all circumstances. The mere fact that we are faithful to God's Word is cause for rejoicing. Troubles and trials merely highlight the great blessing we have.

I think that is why St. Maximilian Kolbe starved to death in Auschwitz with a big smile on his face. He conquered. He was being faithful. That's why Corrie ten Boom endured the worst humiliation, pain, suffering, and degradation in a Nazi concentration camp with good humor and love.

Some of the most remarkable documents of the early church are the letters of St. Ignatius of Antioch, a bishop who was martyred in Rome. The letters were written to various Christian churches as Ignatius was being taken to his death. Everyone knew what was going to happen to him. Ignatius' letters were written in response to Christians who were feeling sorrowful about his fate.

What comes through most strongly is his overwhelming joy at being able to die for Jesus Christ. In fact, he cautions his brothers and sisters not to confuse him by telling him how terrible his impending martyrdom is. These letters are a good illustration of a Christian who is able to find the right expression of joy in the midst of circumstances that are both confusing and trying. Ignatius knew he could be joyful because he was going to win a martyr's crown. At the same time he knew he was weak, and there was always the possibility that he would crumble before the wild beasts. He was glad to have brothers and sisters to pray for him and stand by him, but their expressions of support weren't always helpful.

Think of your own trying and complicated situations. There's something to lament, but there's always something to be joyful about too.

When I first began speaking at conferences thirty-five years ago, there frequently came a time when confusion overwhelmed the overworked organizers—and the poor speakers. I was rushed from one place to another to give a talk at 8:15 in the morning, and then didn't actually get up to speak until 10:00. While I waited, a whole assortment of themes, testimonies, and concerns were introduced by people not scheduled to speak. I was asked to mention different points in my prepared talk. Then I would be asked to shorten the talk because it was getting late and people were tired. Then I was told that a series of people wanted to confer with me after the session. Meanwhile, the program fell further and further behind schedule. Someone would tell me I might go on right now. Then they would say, "No—let's have a few songs to refresh the people first. Father Mike, what songs would you like to have sung?"

At times like these I am not inclined to feel joyful at all. It all seems absurd. I'm thinking of running away.

What am I doing here? What possible good can come out of my contribution?

But wait. There are many things to be joyful about. The conference is part of the great work of renewal God is doing in the church. The conference organizers are doing good work; they'll do better next time. People attending this conference are growing in their spiritual lives and finding fruitful ways to serve others. And these annoying delays and distractions enable other Christians to express their love for the Lord. And what is important is not my prepared talk but the Lord and his work and his glory.

Joy is a matter of perspective. It often takes work. But there are no circumstances of life in which you cannot experience Christian joy. You can experience it as a concrete reality in your life, not just as an abstraction.

That troublesome verse from Philippians—"Rejoice in the Lord always"—is literally true. It's a perfectly rational response to the many things the Lord has done for us. We rejoice because we have a relationship with the Lord Jesus. Look at what he has done for you in this relationship. He has saved you, delivered you from eternal death. He has given you a family, brothers and sisters in the kingdom of God. He has given you hope. He gives you his Word, which reveals God's mind about the way human life should be lived.

Nothing can come between you and the Lord. He brings good out of troubles and trials, and he will never abandon you. He is committed to you. Can you think of a better reason to rejoice?

There is another reason—maybe not a better one, but a sufficient one. We can rejoice because of the good things that happen to other people.

In 1 Corinthians 13, Paul writes that "love does not delight in evil but rejoices in the truth." These are some of the qualities of this rejoicing love: "Love is patient, love is kind, it does not envy, it does not boast. It is not proud. It is not rude. It is not self-seeking, it is not easily angered, it keeps no record of wrong" (13:4-5). In other words, we are becoming loving people to the extent that we rejoice in what is good and true about us and about other people. The selfish person is dejected, envious, and resentful when good things happen to other people. The loving person rejoices. In fact, the loving person has much to rejoice about, because he or she is attuned to the many blessings God is always bestowing on others.

WHERE YOUR HEART IS

How do we handle troubles? Much Christian teaching is aimed at answering that question. Outside the church a whole industry of self-help books and counseling has grown up to help people answer it. We can lay down some general rules, make some useful generalizations, make some shrewd guesses about how to handle personal trials and how not to handle them. But the key is our heart—our inner disposition toward God and others.

In the nineteenth century many families relocated from the Midwest to the South by riverboat. Regional differences were greater in the United States in those days than they are now. Riverboat captains grew accustomed to telling Midwesterners what Southern people were like.

One captain who sailed between Pittsburgh and New Orleans was especially wise. On one trip he picked up a family in Steubenville that was moving to New Orleans.

"What are the people in Louisiana like?" the father of the family asked him.

"What are the people in Ohio like?" the captain asked.

"Oh, they are good people. Caring and generous. We have a lot of good friends in Ohio. If it wasn't for the job situation, we wouldn't be going South."

"Well, I've got good news for you," the captain said. "You'll find that the people in Louisiana are just like that. They are warm and caring and loving. You'll make many fine friends."

Six months later the captain picked up another Ohio family on its way to Louisiana. The father approached him with the same question: "What are the people like down there?" The captain asked his question: "What are the people like in Ohio?"

"Pretty tough to get along with," the man answered. "They tend to be irritable. Sometimes they're mean. We're kind of glad to be leaving."

"Well, the people in Louisiana are just like that," the captain said. "Irritable, hard to get along with, and sometimes mean. You'd better not get your expectations too high."

The captain was never wrong. It always turned out just the way he said. Louisiana people were always like those in Ohio.

Scripture presents Mary as the model of the faithful follower of the Lord who carried the treasures of the kingdom in her heart. She filled her heart with the wonders of God, who had set her aside, who had given her a Son who was the Savior of all humankind, who had made the impossible marriage with Joseph actually happen, who had revealed the future to her, who had rescued her and her family from an evil king, who had destined her to be a woman whom all generations would call blessed. Look at what she could have worried about: the scandal of her impossible pregnancy, finances, her family, the terror of physical danger in the family's escape to Egypt. But Scripture remembers her as a woman who treasured the things of God in her heart and reflected on them. Life was hard. The future was full of foreboding and evil. Mary foresaw this, but her heart was joyful nevertheless.

That is the secret. In the midst of troubles you can be joyful, because you carry the kingdom of God within you.

Facile talk, you say? Words conquering reality?

These are not mere words. The kingdom of God is real. It will stand forever, and it is alive in you now.

"But you don't know what I'm going through."

Right, I don't. Can it be hard? Yes, it can. Can your situation be objectively difficult? Yes. It can be objectively more difficult than the situations of other people you know. You can be afflicted with illness. You can be tormented by emotional problems that make joy seem impossible. You and your family can be starving. You can be beset by terrible frustrations and tragic disappointments.

None of this has to affect your heart. You can guard it, protect it, and continue to experience the joy of the kingdom of God.

That's why Jesus said, "Do not rejoice that the spirits submit to you, but rejoice that your names are written in heaven" (Luke 10:20). The apostles came running in after casting out demons, and Jesus took the wind out of their sails with that remark. Why? Because the basic facts of our fundamental relationship with God are far more reason to rejoice than a few healings. Rejoice that you have been called, that you have responded to the gospel, that you've been saved, redeemed, and loved, that you're destined to live forever in heaven.

Life goes on, nevertheless. Troublesome, distracting, boring, thrilling, disappointing life. Our lives as Christians are largely a matter of preserving the treasures in our heart in the midst of life. Here's how to do it.

GETTING THE VICTORY

First, root out sin. Scripture tells us that if we love the world, there is no room in our heart for God's love (see 1 John 2:15). That's frightening. This warning immediately conjures up an image of the ideal Christian as a man or woman who floats above the things of this world, figuratively if not literally, who is uninvolved in the pleasures and cares of the world, and who thinks of holy things at all times. This is a misleading idea. A Christian does not have to be shut off from the things of the world; at least most Christians are not called that way. However, the world does contain numerous things that will replace the Father's love if we allow them.

The First Letter of John warns us especially about "carnal allurements (2:16)." These are the pleasures of the flesh—food, drink, sex, and the like—that have the capacity to root themselves deeply in our flawed nature and dominate it. They can take control. Ask any alcoholic who knows he's an alcoholic to describe what it's like being in the grip of that addiction. He or she will describe a life that gradually comes to revolve around alcohol. Where will the next drink come from? How's my supply? Will the people we're visiting tonight give me enough to drink?

Christians are not immune to addictions simply by virtue of being Christians. If you have a problem with an addiction, take steps to root it out.

The First Letter of John also warns about "enticements of the eye" and a "life of empty show" (2:16). This is a New Testament passage that is completely up-to-date. It's probably easier to see the truth of this passage in twentieth-century America than it was in first-century Palestine. In those days most people worked so hard to survive that most would have to look long and hard to find enticements of the eye and lives of empty show that would be a danger to them. Today these enticements are all around us. They're a danger to everybody. All we have to do is turn on the television, go to the moves, or pick up a magazine to be tugged by the life of empty show.

What is Scripture really talking about here? I think "enticements of the eye" are novelties, fashions, "the latest." Our life can be driven by the passion to be up-to-date, to see the latest movie, to eat in the hot new restaurant, to know the latest songs and wear the latest clothes, to use the latest computer software, to read the latest book. Even the Christian life can be lived according to what's new. It's a subtle thing. There's nothing wrong with going places and seeing things, and there's value in being alert for better ways to do things. But this can be a problem when a passion for the latest and the trendiest grabs our hearts.

"The life of empty show," I think, is a life driven by the search for compliments. This can be an addiction as alluring as alcohol or drugs. Your life can gradually come to revolve around "looking good." You arrange more and more things in order to parade them in front of other people, to be admired and complimented. When people don't notice you, or don't notice you as much as you think they should—something that will inevitably happen—the black cloud of gloom descends.

There's nothing wrong with compliments. There's nothing wrong with honoring people who deserve honor. But a life dominated by compliments and desire for honors is indeed a life of empty show.

If anything other than the Lord Jesus Christ dominates your heart, root it out. Repent of sin. Change your friends, change your job—do whatever is necessary to deal with allurements, enticements, and temptations.

The sin will return in the form of a temptation, an idea, an option. Resist it. It's harmless as long as it's an idea in your mind. The problem comes when you act on the temptation, when you give in to the lie that this temptation can't be resisted.

Let your heart be filled with the mysteries of God. The greatest mystery is that God loves you. Think about it. God doesn't just love humanity in the abstract, or just Catholics, or just the people in your parish, or just Christians. He loves every human being with an intense personal love. That includes you. He loves you in all your defects, in all your sins, in all your clumsy efforts to love other people and to love him back. He knows exactly how hard you work, how embarrassed you get, how easily you make mistakes. He knows all that and still loves you.

That's why Jesus told his disciples to rejoice because their names were written in heaven. Your name is written in heaven, so rejoice about it. And let God's riches fill your life. He will change you, transform you, show you his victory over stubborn sins and twisted relationships.

The Lord initiated the relationship with you. He will see it through to the end.

You can depend on it.

Chapter Nine

—∿—

THE JOY OF REPENTANCE —THE LORD'S INVITATION

The joy of repentance? Surely I jest, you think. Repentance is like death, taxes, cancer, and other troubles—a nasty fact of life that we must come to terms with. Like trouble, repentance pervades everything. Life is full of trouble; it's full of opportunities to repent too. In fact, there are more opportunities to repent than there is almost anything else to do in life.

How can a nasty, ubiquitous duty like repentance be joyful? Because it brings us to the Lord. Consider this verse from Revelation: "Those whom I love I reprove and chastise; so be zealous and repent" (3:19). The chapter goes on: "Here I am, standing at the door and knocking.

If anyone hears me calling and opens the door, I will go in and dine with him and he with me" (3:20).

Repentance is an invitation, an opening of the door so that the Lord can come in. That's why repentance is joyful. We can speak of repentance as something that brings gladness to our hearts and a smile to our lips because by repenting we open ourselves to the Lord's life-giving grace. When the door is shut, at least part of us is dead inside, without hope. When we open it, we let life in again—through the grace of the Lord Jesus Christ who waits patiently for us to invite him in.

That's why a zealous Christian is eager to repent.

TWO LESSONS OF REPENTANCE

The basic dynamic of repentance is honesty and mercy. Little in our experience in the world equips us to understand this. We learn to give tit for tat, to earn everything we get through our own merits, to avoid unpleasantness, to look good to others in spite of what is really going on, and above all, to be careful. By contrast, the dynamic of the kingdom of God is open and uncomplicated. If we're honest, we experience God's forgiveness. If we forgive, we are forgiven.

I was fortunate to learn some of these lessons in school—particularly in the fourth grade at a boarding school called Coindre Hall.

The school had a set of rules that didn't fit my basic disposition. I especially had difficulty with rules about being quiet. I was a talker. However, the brothers who ran Coindre Hall had a long list of times when silence was required—in the classroom, in the dining hall during prayers, in the library, in the study halls, in the washrooms, and in the dormitories.

I knew these rules, but I continually ignored them. I ignored them so often that at one point I earned the second highest number of demerits for a week's infractions in the history of the school, and all mine were for talking at times when I was supposed to be silent.

This character defect brought me into constant contact with the strong, athletic, blunt, and loving brothers who ran the school. This, in turn, taught me the two main elements of repentance.

From Brother Andre I learned the importance of honesty. He employed then the punishment practices used fifty years ago. Today they are much different. A typical encounter with Brother Andre would go like this.

He would step into the dormitory where the fourth graders slept, and he would say, "Silence. Lights out." The door would close, and the light would snap off. Then I would start in. I always had excellent reasons to talk. I had schoolwork to discuss, games to review, jokes to tell. Suddenly Brother Andre would walk into the dormitory, usually in the middle of one of my loudest laughs. He would come straight to me.

"Did you speak when you weren't supposed to?" he'd ask.

"Yes, Brother."

"Did you know it was wrong to speak at that time?"

"Yes, Brother."

"Come to the front wall."

Once there, he would direct me into the lavatory and say, "Assume the position."

I bent over and grabbed my ankles with my shaking hands. Brother Andre whacked me several times with a paddle. Any boy who had fallen asleep would instantly wake up with those cracks.

In the seconds following those whacks I learned about courage. It was absolutely essential to get back into bed without crying. In front of the others you couldn't show weakness; in bed you could smother the tears in the pillow.

Brother Andre's questions, which I heard so many times, taught me the importance of taking personal responsibility for my behavior. Did you do something wrong? Did you know it was wrong when you did it? I could always give a truckload of extenuating circumstances to explain my actions. But the explanations didn't seem to matter when I stood in front of him. I could have denied my guilt. But what good would that have done? Even if I had managed to fool Brother Andre, I would have had to live with his question ringing in my ears: Did you do something wrong? Of course I did.

I have since come to see that honesty is the antidote for many of the miseries and troubles that afflict us. The truth is that we do sin and we do suffer the consequences of sin. Without God, we learn to avoid and deny these bitter facts. This makes a certain sense: without God there is no forgiveness; without forgiveness there's no reason to repent; without repentance we have every incentive to deny that we are sinners. But with God there is a way out. This is what I learned from Brother Gaspar, the other prefect of discipline at Coindre Hall.

Brother Gaspar would find me in the same situation as Brother Andre, but he would handle it differently.

"Tell me what happened," he'd say.

I would tell him exactly what I did. I wasn't limited to a yes or no answer but I didn't deny that I deserved punishment.

Most of the time Brother Gaspar would let me go without any punishment at all. He was like Jesus with the woman caught in the act of adultery: go and sin no more. Occasionally Brother Gaspar would break the monotony of that, but if he gave me any punishment it would be something to repair the wrong I had done.

Obviously, when I was caught, I preferred to have Brother Gaspar do it than Brother Andre. But the two of them together illustrate the two most important facts about repentance: first, that repentance means embracing responsibility for objective wrongdoing and setting out in a different direction; second, that repentance means throwing ourselves on a God of mercy, who always forgives.

ADMITTING OUR GUILT

First, the Brother Andre lesson: repentance is acknowledgment of objective wrongdoing. The word *repentance* in Aramaic means "to turn around completely"—to change, to reverse, to go from something to something else. In the case of sinful behavior, it means turning from wrongdoing to virtue, from Satan to God. Repentance is a realistic, objective process that involves getting off one path and onto another.

We tend to think of repentance as an emotional state. It may involve emotions, but the essence of it is deciding to get off one path and onto another. If we understand that, we are much more likely to step out of the troublesome, dangerous, wrong things that make our lives so miserable. In fact, our sins become opportunities for grace. That's why it is important to squarely face what we've done wrong.

Our inclination, on the other hand, is to rationalize. You know how it goes. Our sin is always an extraordinary circumstance that is accompanied by an amazingly convincing set of mitigating circumstances. God never foresaw the irresistible power of the temptation inflicted on me when he decreed that the thing I did is a sin. The circumstances were so complex that I was virtually forced to lie, to cheat, and so on.

The truth is that God doesn't care where you were. He cares about where you are going. If you spend your time and energy worrying about, regretting, justifying, explaining, and mitigating behavior that is objectively wrong, you won't be able to change it. Only God can change it, and he requires that you admit that your behavior is objectively wrong.

It took me a long time to learn the lesson Brother Andre taught me at Coindre Hall; not even a succession of painful paddlings was enough to curb my unruly tongue. It was a problem for many years.

I faced up to it some years ago when I examined the way I talked about the Franciscan friars I lived with. I enjoyed talking about these fine men in terms of gentle, casual mockery. I made fun of their idiosyncrasies. I made jokes about their weaknesses. I'd kid the men who slept in, who were sloppy, who ate too much. I thought it was playful kidding, good clean fun. But then I noticed that the laughter was hollow when I kidded them that way. I saw that what I was doing was wrong. Under the guise of good clean fun, I was running down their reputations and holding qualities that they were not proud of up to public ridicule. This negative approach to humor wasn't humor at all.

When these ideas first occurred to me, my impulse was to object. My heart was good. All I was doing was trying to lighten up a household of men who sometimes took things too seriously. I didn't mean to hurt anybody. But I clearly heard God say, "But what you *did* was wrong. Now repent and change."

End of discussion. I did repent, and through God's grace, I did change. I still have a taste for negative humor, and I constantly deal with temptations to show how good I can be at it. But my brothers in the monastery don't have to force a smile when I walk into the room now.

That's the first element in repentance—the Brother Andre lesson. To repent we first need to take responsibility for our actions when we see that they are wrong. We need to turn, to change, and not to worry about excusing ourselves or getting distracted into sideline issues.

Maybe the atmosphere at home does need lightening. Maybe people are too thin-skinned. Maybe the way we speak isn't so *very* wrong. But if it is wrong, change it.

GOD'S GIFT

The second element in repentance is the joyous part. Repentance is a gift from God. It's a grace. We cannot repent on our own power any more than we can undo the effects of sin in our lives on our own power. But God can, and God does. He gives us the grace to change when we ask him for it. He really does obliterate our offenses and free us and those around us from their effects.

This is the joy of repentance.

The grace to repent is an often-neglected gift of the Holy Spirit. The Holy Spirit came for many reasons—to console us, to be our advocate, to teach us all truth, to guide us. But he also came to convict us of sin. When Peter prayed for the Spirit to fall at the house of the Gentile Cornelius, he prayed for the gift of *metanoia*— the gift of life-giving repentance.

This suggests how closely repentance is bound into the very act of becoming a Christian. When the Jews asked Peter what they had to do to be saved, he said, "Repent, and be baptized, then you will receive the Holy Spirit" (Acts 2:38). It's really all one thing; the acknowledgment of our wrongdoing puts us in a position of surrender before God. He sends the Holy Spirit, which includes the gift of life-giving repentance.

John said that Jesus would send a baptism with the Holy Spirit and fire. When we come to Jesus, he purifies. The purifying fire of the Holy Spirit makes us clean. It brings the impurities in us out into the light, scorches them, and thus makes us strong. We become "dead to sin, but living for God in Christ Jesus" (Romans 6:11).

We need to learn to see this continuing process of purification as the gift that it is. It is the perfect antidote to depression and self-pity. How do you feel when you do something wrong: when you let someone down, or relapse into a bad habit you thought you had conquered, or tell a lie, or say something mean, or neglect a commitment? Most likely, you feel terrible. Here you are, making your own personal contribution to the store of trouble in the world, even as you weep and wail about the trouble that makes your life tougher.

Take heart. Failures are opportunities to improve. You can't get better until you see what's wrong. This is not a platitude or some attempt to put a happy face on a sad situation. It's the literal truth. One of the reasons why the Holy Spirit has been given to us is to lead us to repentance.

Sin is sad. Sinning is no fun. Sin weighs us down spiritually and emotionally. Repenting is the opposite of the oppression of sin. Repentance sets us free. Repentance is joyful.

I see this all the time when I hear confessions. Much of the time I can hear the difference before and after absolution in the person's voice. This is the audible difference between oppression and freedom, between death and life, between sorrow and joy.

THREE LEVELS OF REPENTANCE

It's sometimes difficult to understand repentance because sin can be complicated to untangle. There are different levels of repentance, just as there are different levels of sin. Repentance operates differently in our lives depending on the way sin does.

The First Level Is Direct Repentance for Sin that We Intentionally Committed. This is the kind of sin—and the kind of repentance—we are most familiar with. This is the way I sinned when I mocked my fellow friars at home. We can all list dozens of specific sins that we deliberately set out to commit. We act selfishly; we lust; we're resentful; we're jealous and envious; we don't honor commitments we have made.

Repentance for these offenses is a relatively straightforward business. When you become aware of the sin, repent. Don't pass over it. Don't tell yourself you'll pray and fast more and hope it will get better. Just tell the Lord you're sorry and ask forgiveness. That's the way to deal with intentional sins.

The Second Level of Repentance Involves "Root Sins." By this I mean the core of disorder and wrongdoing in our lives that we are not aware of—or only vaguely aware of. Here is where the business of repentance can get a little complicated.

Many of our sins are rooted in unconscious patterns of thinking and acting. Some of these patterns can be traced to our childhood homes. If you grew up in a home where your parents severely corrected every little mistake, you may as an adult be continually dissatisfied and have a tendency to demand too much of others. You aren't really going to deal with the sin in your life unless you deal with the root pattern.

Some people have a biochemical imbalance that causes them to be depressed, anxious, or fearful. Their lives are full of pain, and nothing much improves until they can get rid of the underlying problem. Some people are in bondage to evil spirits. The spirits have a hold on their lives that makes it impossible to deal definitively with sin by using simple repentance. Some people's relationship with God is defective in such a way that it twists their relationships with people.

I remember one woman who appeared to be a fervent committed Christian but who had a number of difficulties. She would nag her husband and children. She was terribly anxious about the future. She wanted total financial security against all possible developments. She wanted to personally make every decision affecting her life, or at least have veto power over others' decisions. She wanted to control everything and was very unhappy when, as often happened, she couldn't.

At the same time, she prayed every day, went to church, gave her time to help others. She appeared to be a strong Christian with patterns of sin that strong Christians shouldn't have to put up with.

Her problem was a spiritual one: she hadn't really given control of her life to God. She came to see that she had tried to strike a bargain with him. She would do all the "religious things"—even many more religious things than "necessary"—if only she could run the rest of her life with God's help. Of course, she didn't put it in those terms, but that was the character of her spiritual life.

The lady experienced tremendous freedom when she was able to face this problem and eventually turn her life over to God. Those around her experienced freedom too. She didn't have to nag her husband and children to perform flawlessly. Anxiety about money and the future melted away. Her root sin had been uprooted.

This woman's root sin was pride—the greatest of all the capital sins, the deepest and most tenacious root of all. When we put ourselves at the center of our lives, nothing else is going to quite measure up to the wonderful person sitting on the throne. Some people and circumstances will fall a little bit short; most will fall way short. Once we are in this situation, the sin of pride will lead us into many other sins. Until pride is handled, until the self is gone and Jesus is on the throne, sin will continue to plague us.

The Third Level of Repentance Is Progressive. We only become aware of the need to repent when we are advancing in the spiritual life. There are areas of our lives not in right order; indeed, they are objectively sinful, even though we can't point to specific acts where we're guilty.

For example, your relationship with your brother isn't going right. It's full of tension, suspicion, unhappiness. But you can't see any specific sins on either side to repent of. The situation is wrong; it's sinful. But it's not at all clear how repentance applies to it.

Or you think that perhaps your life is not given over to the Lord in some important, fundamental way. You don't do enough for the poor and needy. Your time is too taken up with your own concerns. You think that God is calling you to something deeper and that you are resisting him.

I call this level of repentance "enlightenment." These problems are not something that you can define easily; they don't jump out at you as you review the Ten

Commandments in an examination of conscience. They dawn on you. They're part of your nature that has yet to be fully redeemed in Christ. We rarely see these problems until we've gotten serious about following the Lord. As C. S. Lewis once said, we don't know how bad we are until we try to be good.

Paul was talking about this enlightenment in Romans 12:2: "Do not be conformed to the pattern of this world," he wrote, "but be transformed by the renewal of your mind, that you may test and approve what is the will of God, his good, pleasing, and perfect will."

When our minds start to change, we see new possibilities of change in our lives. We're able to see the perfect will of God. This change in our minds often comes as a sudden revelation; it often comes as a gradual understanding.

A relationship with a pastoral counselor can be helpful. So is regular use of the sacrament of reconciliation. Frequently in confession people say, "I don't do anything wrong." They are talking about obvious sins—cheating, lust, lying, and the like. But as we talk, it gradually becomes clear that something is lacking in the spiritual dimension of their lives. Nothing is wrong because they don't look at anything with spiritual eyes.

With spiritual eyes we can see the spiritual ways we fall short. Are we grateful to God? Do we follow him zealously? Is our prayer really fervent?

The great exemplar for the third level of repentance is Peter, the rock. Peter strikes me as the patron saint of Christians with unrenewed minds. He blundered and blustered, saying whatever came into his head more often than not. To me, the fact that the Christian Scriptures portray the first head of the church in such an unflattering light is further proof that Christianity was founded by God.

The story that is especially germane here is Peter's vigorous defense of his master. Peter was the most zealous follower of Jesus, until Jesus said he was going to Jerusalem to be killed by his enemies. Peter jumped up. "No. I will never let it happen" (Matthew 16:22). In effect, you'll go to Jerusalem over my dead body.

A perfectly understandable, even admirable, reaction. Exactly what a loyal follower would be expected to do. Only Jesus responded with a fierce rebuff. "Out of my sight, Satan. You are thinking the thoughts of man, not of God" (Mark 8:33). It took Peter a long time to make the shift from man's thoughts to God's. He repented, and repented again. He denied his master in Jerusalem, repented, and was not present at the cross.

But Peter did learn. According to Christian tradition, he faced the same circumstances in later life that Jesus faced in Galilee. Peter was head of the church in Rome when persecution erupted. The authorities came after him, and Peter headed out of town. On the way, Jesus appeared to him.

"Where are you going, Peter?" he asked.

Peter explained about the cruel emperor and the savage beasts and the certainty that the head of the Christians in Rome would be killed.

And Jesus explained that he was heading to Rome and so should Peter. And Peter did turn around and head back. Tradition holds that he was crucified like his master, only upside down.

We will learn too as we persevere through sin and trouble. Jesus explained the goal of repentance when he told the disciples that he was going to die. In Luke 9 he said: "If any want to become my followers, let them deny themselves and take up their cross daily and follow me" (9:23, NRSV).

This often-quoted verse offers a rich image of the faithful Christian rising from his or her bed each morning and embracing the miseries of the day. The more miserable the miseries the better. But surely Jesus' command is clear. By nature we live our lives in a way that centers on ourselves. Jesus tells us to live for him and for others. This is not an intellectual proposition or a one-time dramatic conversion decision. It is something we demonstrate with our lives, and it's something we do every day.

When Jesus says, "Take up your cross daily," he doesn't mean only, "Put up with irritations and bad weather and missed appointments." He means, "Do as I did. Put yourself to death. Become someone who no longer lives for yourself, but for me and all for whom I live. Join with my suffering and death, make your cross a cross of redemption, die as I died so others might find eternal life."

Every little act of repentance is part of the big decision to live for God. Repentance builds strength and fidelity into our character. It makes us into the kind of people for whom troubles are opportunities to grow in holiness, to give glory to God, to witness that our treasure is not in this world but in the kingdom of God.

In fact, the path to heaven is strewn with little acts of repentance that serve as road markers on our journey home. Take that path and you will find joy—and glory.

Epilogue

—ⵡ—

Many would call it trouble. It is weakness and even a form of sickness, but what kind of trouble is it? I am writing about my own condition which developed in my seventy-third year. It is a form of polyneuropathy, which is still a new name to me.

Because of muscle weakness, fatigue spells, and respiratory contraction, I have canceled all travel for purposes of speaking or board meetings. My condition could improve, or it could worsen. It is an inherited condition present in the male members of my family.

But what kind of trouble is it? I pray more now that I am not traveling and have more time to rest. I do more spiritual reading. I see more students for spiritual direction and personal ministry. I even preach and teach more often on campus. My deepest desire in ministry is to be a shepherd or spiritual father to our students. My life has been blessed with peace and joy.

What a blessing! In the Epilogue of the first edition of this book, published in 1989, I wrote from the Youngstown jail where I was incarcerated for demonstrating in front of an abortion clinic. I wrote that I was peaceful then because I knew I was in love with Jesus Christ, and he would not abandon me.

That is true now. My prayer each day is launched on three verses of Scripture: "To be near God is my happiness" (Psalm 73:28); "Offer your body as a living sacrifice to God" (Romans 12:1); and "Dedicate your life to thankfulness" (Colossians 3:15). If my happiness is being near God, there is no reason for other things to make me unhappy. If I am to offer my body as a living sacrifice, there is no reason for me to be concerned about the growing weaknesses in my body. If I dedicate my life to gratefulness to God for all his mercy and blessings in my life and service, there is no room to complain or be resentful.

I still struggle with many things. I am a sinner desperate for God's unending mercy. I am not looking for more trouble, but I believe in St. Paul's cry amidst persecution, "Who will separate us from the love of Christ?" (Romans 8:35, NRSV). By God's mercy, may it never be trouble that comes between us and the Lord of all.

Notes

—〰—

Chapter One
Peace and Trouble—the Missing Link

1. St. Augustine, "On Pastors" (Sermon 46, 10-11: CCL 41, 536-538). *The Liturgy of the Hours*, vol. 4. (New York: Catholic Book Publishing Company, 1975), 276.

Chapter Two
Welcome to Trouble—and Deeper Intimacy with Jesus

1. Pope John Paul II, *Letter of the Supreme Pontiff John Paul II to All the Priests of the Church on the Occasion of Holy Thursday 1979*. L'Osservatore Romano, English edition, 17 April 1979, #10.
2. *Ibid*.
3. Alban Goodier, *A More Excellent Way* (St. Meinrad, Ind.: Abbey Press Publications, 1964), 17.

Chapter Four
The Trouble Is in Your Head

1. C. S. Lewis, *Christian Reflections* (Grand Rapids, Mich.: Wm. B. Eerdmans, 1967), xi.
2. Harry Blamires, a student of C. S. Lewis, was present when Lewis made the remarks about the dead atheist and the World War I poets. Blamires relayed the anecdotes to Jim Manney.
3. C. S. Lewis, *The Weight of Glory and Other Addresses* (New York: MacMillan Publishing Company, 1980, revised and expanded edition), 18-19.
4. St. Gregory Nazianzen, "Oratio 14—De pauperum amore," (23-25: PG 35, 887-890), *The Liturgy of the Hours*, vol. 2 (New York: Catholic Book Publishing Company, 1976), 96.
5. From the writings of St. Rose of Lima, Ad medicum Castillo: edit. L. Getino, La Patrona de America, Madrid, 1928. *Liturgy of the Hours*, vol. 4 (New York: Catholic Book Publishing Company, 1975), 1342-1343.

Chapter Five
You Really Do Have an Enemy

1. According to The American Chesterton Society's Web site, "This story has been repeated so often about Chesterton that we suspect it is true. Also, it seems it is never told about anyone other than Chesterton. What we have not found, however, is any documentary evidence for it." The Society points out that the reply is typical of Chesterton's humility and wit and is associated with the title of his book, *What's Wrong with the World*. As quoted on www.chesterton.org. Accessed November 11, 2004.

Chapter Seven
Walking in Faith and Discerning God's Will

1. Walter M. Abbot, S.J., ed., "Dogmatic Constitution on the Church," *The Documents of Vatican II* (New York: Guild Press, America Press, Association Press, copyright 1966 by The America Press), #10, 27.
2. Abbot, #12, 30.
3. Abbot, #12, 30.
4. Pope John Paul II, *Christifideles Laici, Post-Synodal Apostolic Exhortation Of His Holiness On The Vocation And The Mission Of The Lay Faithful In The Church And In The World*, #24.
5. "Decree on the Apostolate of the Laity," *The Documents of Vatican Council II*, #3, 492.

6. St. Polycarp, "The Epistle of Polycarp to the
    Philippians" (Cap. 1, 1-2, 3: Funk 1, 267-269), *The
    Liturgy of the Hours*, vol. 4 (New York: Catholic
    Book Publishing Company, 1975), 315.